ELLEN ELLIOTT

GEEK
AND YE
SHALL FIND

HARVEST HOUSE PUBLISHERS
EUGENE, OREGON

Scripture quotations are taken from the Holy Bible, New Living Translation, copyright © 1996, 2004, 2015 by Tyndale House Foundation. Used by permission of Tyndale House Publishers, Inc., Carol Stream, Illinois 60188. All rights reserved.

Cover by Bryce Williamson

Cover photo © artisteer/ Getty Images

Interior illustrations by Ellen Elliott

Geek and Ye Shall Find
Copyright © 2019 by Ellen Matkowski
Published by Harvest House Publishers
Eugene, Oregon 97408
www.harvesthousepublishers.com

ISBN 978-0-7369-7634-3 (pbk.)
ISBN 978-0-7369-7635-0 (eBook)

Library of Congress Cataloging-in-Publication Data

Names: Elliott, Ellen, author.
Title: Geek and ye shall find / Ellen Elliott.
Description: Eugene, Or. : Harvest House Publishers, 2019. | Includes
    bibliographical references.
Identifiers: LCCN 2018038721 (print) | LCCN 2018061379 (ebook) | ISBN
    9780736976350 (ebook) | ISBN 9780736976343 (pbk.)
Subjects: LCSH: Christian life. | Bible stories. | Science fiction--Religious
    aspects.
Classification: LCC BV4515.3 (ebook) | LCC BV4515.3 .E45 2019 (print) | DDC
    242--dc23
LC record available at https://lccn.loc.gov/2018038721

Printed in the United States of America

19 20 21 22 23 24 25 26 27 / VP-SK / 10 9 8 7 6 5 4 3 2 1

ACKNOWLEDGMENTS

So many thanks...

...to my family (Anna, Noah, Dad, Mom, Karen, Bill, Henry, Oliver, Sara, Bobby), who never forced me to play sports.

...to my amazing agent, Rachel Orr at Prospect Agency, who reins in my crazy.

...to the splendid people at Harvest House Publishers, who took a chance on this book.

...to my fact-checking Geek Brigade, who attempted to save me from potential tar-and-feathering from the geek community: Bill Skaggs, Phil Gilbreath, Vu Ha, Christina Larsen, Amy Malaise (aka Malady,) Megan Harwell, Wesley Rice, Emily Moore, Jim Austin, Robyn Wall.

...and to my cats, Levi and Fey, who contributed absolutely nothing.

CONTENTS

THE-INTRODUCTION-THAT-MUST-NOT-BE-NAMED

I am a geek. I've been a geek since I was a young child…raised on the farmlands of Kansas by my humble, adoptive earth parents, eventually learning to use my secret superpowers for the good of humanity. (Just kidding. That's the beginning of *Superman*. My childhood is not as interesting. I have no superpowers. But I did live in Kansas once.)

Growing up, I was deeply passionate about myriad interests. When I fell for a new one, I fell *hard*. I adored superheroes, *Ripley's Believe It or Not!*, *Bloom County*, and *Far Side* cartoons—as well as prancing around in my red pajamas like *The Greatest American Hero*. When I was on the color guard squad, I once sewed a bat flag and tried to persuade my band director to let us perform a *Batman*-themed flag-line routine.[1] I also watched *Sesame Street* waaaaaaay past the time my peers moved on to music videos, mainly because I was still obsessed with Super Grover. (Honestly, my Muppet devotion has yet to waver. I would still choose meeting Animal over a human rock star any day of the week.)

I didn't care if my passions were cool or not. I loved what I loved, and I wanted to share my enthusiasm with anyone who would listen.

---

1. My attempt was fruitless. We still marched to Sousa. But I blame my poor sewing skills and not my geeky gumption.

What constitutes an official geek seems to be a point of controversy. Some people think a geek is someone who's good with technology or owns a massive comic book collection. Others believe a geek must attend Comic-Con to be legit. I'm always a sap for dictionary definitions, and *Merriam-Webster's* says the original meaning of *geek* was "a carnival performer often billed as a wild man whose act usually includes biting the head off a live chicken or snake."[2]

Ick.

Sorry, that's not much help.

Personally, I think becoming a geek today is simple. Find something you're passionate about and embrace it wholeheartedly. That's it; it's not that complicated.

I also think being a geek can walk hand in hand with being a Christian. We Christians, too, are fervent and devoted, and we want to share our passion with the rest of the universe.

You don't have to possess an official title to be a Christian, or be a trained theologian (I'm certainly not). You don't have to prove your legitimacy to anyone. You just have to accept God's gift of love and salvation through His Son, Jesus Christ. That's it. It's a soul-altering choice, but it's also not complicated.

• • •

I need to share a few caveats before you go on in this book, to ward off potential author hate mail:

First, expect **spoilers**. You should pretty much assume this book is one big spoiler. Please don't write me an irate letter because I ruined the ending of *The Muppet Movie* for you. Come on, spoiler phobes. The movie was released in 1979. You've had time.

Second, some of the movies and television shows referenced do contain some **violence, naughty words, smooching, and other such**

---

2. The real question here is: when does a person decide that live chicken head-biting is a skill they might possess? That was not a chapter in my junior high Career Orientation class. Are there internships for that sort of occupation?

shenanigans.[3] Sigh. Yes, I know that's problematic, this being a Christian book and all. I'm also aware that some Christians will think I'm bordering on heresy by including a zombie chapter in a devotional, but hear me out.

I don't think we can necessarily lump material into Christian or non-Christian, approved or not approved, safe or not safe categories. Just open the Bible and read some stories. Whoa, Nelly! Talk about violence and passion. If you created a realistic movie portrayal of the life of David, it would be rated R, without a doubt. His story has *everything*: adultery, assassination, beheading. But that isn't to say David's story isn't of immense value to us. His life provides powerful teachings about loyalty, heroism, repentance, and forgiveness.

I believe we can also draw spiritual lessons from movies, television shows, comic books, and games, even though we might have to wade through a little bit of spiciness to get there.

Consider *Little Shop of Horrors*. My mom *tisk-tisked* me for including the musical in this book. She heartily disapproves of Audrey II's attitude, foul mouth, and murderous streak. "That *plant*," scolded my mother as she shook her head at me, as though I had joined a drug cartel. But I overrode her protests because, well, Audrey II's vile behavior is the point. That plant is just plain evil. She's the *villain*, and the truth is, villains are real too. Sometimes learning how to identify them in fiction can help us identify them in real life.

Yet we need to know our boundaries.

A friend once pointed out to me that the armor of God, described in Ephesians 6:10-17, doesn't include pants. It includes a helmet, a sword, a breastplate, a shield...there's even a belt. But no pants. Common sense would say that if you're to wear a belt, you should also wear pants. That's why I believe that, in addition to wearing our armor of God every day, we're supposed to put on our Pants of Common Sense.

When we're deciding what to put into our brains, those pants tell

---

3. As far as naughty words go—frankly, I find most cursing just plain lazy. It's easy to glom onto one of the standard ten or so curse words, but many *other* words are out there. Millions! It takes a lot more creativity to come up with something like "frizzfrazzling" or "Oh, my appendix!" I just think writers need to be more creative.

us there's some stuff we shouldn't be watching, like pornography, ultra-violent movies and video games, and material that ridicules or demeans Jesus. For stuff like that, the pants say, "Nope."

We also need to consider our personal strengths and weaknesses. Material that might not be a stumbling block for someone else might be a stumbling block for you. For instance, if you struggle with lusty thoughts, you probably need to stay clear of Slave Princess Leia conventions, if you know what I mean. Know your weaknesses. Guard your heart and mind.

With all that said, I hope you enjoy *Geek and Ye Shall Find*. I certainly enjoyed writing it for you.

Much love,
Ellen

1

TAKE NOTICE
LOST

Don't look out only for your own interests,
but take an interest in others, too.

PHILIPPIANS 2:4

How often do people get stranded on a desert island for real? Judging from books, television, and movies, we're setting ourselves up for it anytime we leave the house. Consider *Gilligan's Island, Robinson Crusoe, Swiss Family Robinson,*[1] *Cast Away, Lord of the Flies, Island of the Blue Dolphins*, and probably enough romance novels to fill the Smithsonian.

I don't like my chances of desert-island survival, mainly because I can never decide on an answer to that age-old question, "If you could have only one item with you when stranded alone on a desert island, what would it be?"

Obviously, a smart answer would be "a boat." But that seems like cheating. I don't like cheating, but I also don't like useless answers, like "a Parcheesi set." I usually say, "Let me ponder that thought-provoking question," and then I blurt, "Hey, look, a frozen yogurt shop!" After that, the other person drops the subject.

I get it, though. For some reason, the thought of being trapped on a desert island with only minimal resources and our wits is fascinating

---

1. Apparently, you should be especially concerned if your name is Robinson.

to most of us—which is probably why the television series *Lost* was such a huge hit.

Lost is the story of some strangers stranded on a mysterious island after a plane crash, where the main characters eventually become close-knit. The show focuses on Jack (the troubled, handsome doctor), Kate (the troubled, beautiful prisoner), Sawyer (the troubled, rugged con man), Hurley (the troubled, lovable lottery winner), Locke (the troubled, suddenly non-paralytic nutcase), Sayid (the troubled, sweetheart torturer), Claire (the troubled, pregnant Aussie), Charlie (the troubled, charming rock star), and Sun and Jin (the troubled, Korean mafia couple).

Most of the episodes explore the island's history and secrets, as well as show detailed flashbacks from one of the main character's lives prior to the plane crash. As the characters, always flawed but likable, slowly work through past mistakes toward personal redemption, they also learn character-building lessons. In addition, they become a makeshift family.

But I'm not going to write about any of those people.

You see, *many* passengers survived the plane crash and became part of the beach-dwelling tribe destined to inhabit the island. The extra survivors, however, were usually part of the literal background in most scenes, not really noticed by the main characters or viewers.

In Season 3, the *Lost* writers decided to shake things up. Enter Nicki and Paulo. Well, not really "enter." They'd been on the island the entire time. We just never noticed.

Suddenly, our *Lost* world had new main characters. Granted, we soon found out Nicki and Paulo were despicable people (quite unlikable). Yet, Nicki was nice to look at, and Paulo was...well, equally nice to look at. That was pretty much all they had going for them. In typical flashback fashion, we were told Nicki and Paulo had quite the past. Not only were they thieves and murderers, but they also didn't feel too bad about it. They were nothing like our lovable Hurley.

Lost fans hated the characters so much that they began harassing the writers to get rid of them. The writers finally devoted one last episode to Nicki and Paulo, wherein they died horrible deaths, even by *Lost* standards.

Nicki and Paulo were not a success story. Nevertheless, I give the writers credit for opening our eyes. I hadn't thought that much about all those other people stranded on the island. Everything was all about troubled Jack and troubled Kate and troubled Sawyer and troubled Hurley and troubled Locke and troubled Sayid and troubled Claire and troubled Charlie and troubled Sun and troubled Jin. Over and over and over.

With the screen so dominated by the main characters, it was easy to forget the minor characters. But all of the characters had their own history, secrets, struggles, fears, and joys. It turns out the island was *filled* with main characters. We just focused on only a few of them.

● ● ●

How often do we do exactly that—fail to focus on people in the background of our own lives?

A while back, I worked at a thrift store part-time. I learned many a valuable (and often weird) lesson in that year—like don't stick your hand into a donated ski hat because it might be full of unexplainable goo, and, yes, a live cat may very well be in that donated cat carrier. But no lesson was as valuable as the one I learned because of Jane Smith.[2]

My assigned thrift store area was the book section. Boxes full of donated books poured into the back room, and I opened each one for sorting. One day something caught my eye along with the books: photos of a young, smiling, blond mom with her baby.

Now, when you work in a thrift store, you quickly learn that almost anything can and will be donated: mismatched socks, broken plates, half-eaten cans of Pringles—mine eyes have seen it all. One thing you *don't* typically see, however, are baby pictures. Most moms hold those suckers tighter than a guinea pig with a carrot. When I saw a pile of those precious baby photos, my mommy Spidey senses started tingling, and I studied the mom holding her baby. Judging by the style of her

---

2. Not her real name. Her real last name was far more memorable, like Smithkowski or Smithsmithysmitherson.

clothing, the photos were probably just a few years old. Why would this mom give away her precious baby's photos?

I opened more of the woman's boxes, many of them large, and found a few other items that registered trouble on my radar: her name-engraved, childhood baby cradle; her entire collection of underwear; high school yearbooks; and a list of possible names for her baby. When a fellow employee and I found her purse, complete with money and ID, I knew something was wrong in the life of Miss Jane Smith. You don't end up with all your life's possessions sitting on a thrift store sorting table if things are hunky-dory.

"Well, who knows?" said the fellow employee. "Just tuck her purse, yearbooks, and photos in the corner, and if she comes for them, give those back to her. Sell everything else."

But I couldn't sell any of it. I kept looking at that young mom holding her baby so tightly. Something had happened to this woman, and I might currently be the only person who cared enough to find out what it was and get her belongings back to her.

I started snooping, as I am wont to do, and I found the truck pickup crew who emptied her place. After much prodding, they remembered that Jane's landlord told them he'd discovered her apartment had been abandoned for more than a month. One crew member said her purse was just sitting on the kitchen table. I groaned. My quest was not boding well.

I began digging through her things again. If snooping is a fine art, I'm the Leonardo da Vinci of nosing around. I found her waitressing apron from a nearby restaurant. I deduced that she was a fairly recent graduate of the local high school, a nursing school dropout, and the owner of a run-down Toyota. I slowly began to piece together a life: She liked to write poetry. She loved her child. She was going through a rough time. She was sad.

I finally managed to track down a phone number for her parents.

"Hello, Mrs. Smith? Are you the mother of Jane?" I asked the woman who answered.

Pause.

"Yes..." she answered cautiously.

"I'm at the thrift store, and I have all of Jane's belongings here."

"Oh, my…Well, I'll come get them."

"Um, Mrs. Smith?"

"Yes?"

"Is Jane okay?"

I learned that Jane had been in rehab for the past month, trying to straighten out her life. Her child was with the father. Her mother had no clue her apartment had been cleared out. When Mrs. Smith came by later that day, I handed her the handful of baby photos, and she looked at them wistfully.

"Thank you," she said. "This will mean a lot to Jane."

I still don't know much about Jane, but I do know she's a main character. And she's not the only main character out there.

That crosswalk guard, that bank teller, that homeless woman…all the people you meet are the main character in their own life. They have a story. God created them. They're important to Him, and they were created special. Psalm 139:13-14 says, "You made all the delicate, inner parts of my body and knit me together in my mother's womb. Thank you for making me so wonderfully complex! Your workmanship is marvelous—how well I know it."

Sometimes it's hard to notice others. We get stuck in our own story, our own life, and our own head. But life is not all about us, and sometimes we need the Holy Spirit to give us a nudge. He may whisper to us,

Ask her how her day is going.

Smile at him.

Ask her if she needs help.

Tell her she's beautiful.

We need to notice the people around us because it might make all the difference in the world to them, to those main characters. We don't know what the end of their story will be. We may never know. I don't know what happened to Jane Smith, but I know she'll have her underwear, her baby photos, and her purse, and somehow that might make a difference in her story.

Look around. See who's there. Be kind and make a difference.

2

PROTECTION
COSPLAY

Put on all of God's armor
so that you will be able to stand firm
against all strategies of the devil.

EPHESIANS 6:11

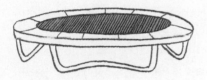

I've always enjoyed a good dress-up, starting when I was a child.

Thankfully, wearing a costume is socially acceptable for children. They have lots of opportunities to do it, like holidays, book-character days, and playdates full of make-believe. My friends and I were particularly fond of donning old 1970s thrift store floral dresses and playing *Little House on the Prairie*. (I always got stuck being Mary.) And in elementary school, even that kid who sometimes showed up to class wearing a cape was generally given a free pass.

For teenagers, though, it gets a little tougher to do the dress-up thing without scrutiny. I think that's why I gravitated toward theater during those years. I could still play dress-up, but technically I was "acting." In those performances, I got to be everything from a bank robber to a chicken to a lamp.[1]

As an adult, though, it's tough to get away with dressing up. Walking into a bank as the Terminator (or even as a lamp) is going to get you some looks. Or maybe arrested.

---

1. I was never that great at acting, but I was a terrific lamp.

I think that's why cosplay was invented. (I don't know why it was so important to smush the words *costume play* into *cosplay*, but apparently that extra syllable was just too exhausting.)

Anyway, cosplay is a hobby where people dress up in costumes. That's basically it. I've noticed that we geeks like to make up official names for simple things that don't necessarily need them.

The first recorded example of cosplaying was in 1908. At an Ohio skating rink masquerade, Mr. and Mrs. William A. Fell dressed as the popular sci-fi comic characters Mr. Skygack from Mars and Miss Dillpickles, who might have the best names in the history of science fiction. Or maybe ever. I'm now kicking myself for not naming my kids Skygack and Dillpickles.

From there, cosplaying has progressed from just putting on a flour sack and calling yourself an alien to a huge global phenomenon.

Cosplayers often dress up as a specific character from a comic book, movie, television show, manga, or video game. Any character you can geek out over, you can cosplay. Other cosplayers choose to create their own characters. Costumes can be as simple as pasting an *S* on your chest and calling yourself Superman, or as elaborate as creating a nearly functioning Iron Man costume. Some might take a character from one genre and add a fresh spin on it, like making a steampunk version of Mary Poppins or a Jabba the Hutt fairy. With cosplay, your costume is limited only by your own imagination.

Cosplayers can spend hours, weeks, or even months creating and modifying materials for their perfect costume. They use hair dye or wigs, neon contact lenses, body paint, and even tattoos. They can become experts with Styrofoam, fiberglass, latex, woodworking, and welding. Some cosplayers even get so good at creating costumes and fake weaponry that they turn their skill into a full-time profession.

Once cosplayers have developed their costumes, they attend fan conventions to show off their masterpieces, sometimes acting out their character mannerisms with other cosplayers. They often participate in competitions at cosplay festivals, conventions, and Renaissance Faires, where they're judged on presentation, accuracy, and craftsmanship.

Rules of cosplay have been developed through the years, mainly because of questionable cosplayer antics. A "no costume is no costume" rule means that if you're naked, that's just what you are—naked. You're not Lady Godiva. You're just naked. And probably about to be arrested, to go sit in a jail cell with the banking Terminator. There's also a "no fire" rule (the qualifying event must have been spectacular to observe). You can't bring real weapons. And a rancid peanut butter incident resulted in a "no messy substances" rule.

It's astounding to see how much time, energy, and creativity a cosplayer will spend on a costume. Inspiring, really. But cosplay got me thinking: What if we Christians spent even a fraction of the same devotion each day to clothing ourselves spiritually?

I think it would change our lives.

• • •

Life is difficult. It would be nice if we could jump out of bed every morning and sashay through our day without a care, but that's not how the world works. As Christians, we're living in a spiritual battlefield 24 hours a day. Satan is fighting to destroy our relationship with God and to get the upper hand in our lives. We're constantly pummeled with his false messages, lies, and temptations as he tries to tear us away from our first love: God.

A war is going on, whether or not we're aware of it, and our hearts and souls are on the line.

So, then, how should we spiritually protect ourselves every day?

Thankfully, to find a solution, we don't have to spend as much time rummaging in our Bibles as we might have to rummage in our closets every morning. In Ephesians 6:10-17, Paul describes the battle armor we need to don:

> A final word: Be strong in the Lord and in his mighty power. Put on all of God's armor so that you will be able to stand firm against all strategies of the devil. For we are not fighting against flesh-and-blood enemies, but against evil rulers and authorities of the unseen world, against mighty

powers in this dark world, and against evil spirits in the heavenly places.

Therefore, put on every piece of God's armor so you will be able to resist the enemy in the time of evil. Then after the battle you will still be standing firm. Stand your ground, putting on the belt of truth and the body armor of God's righteousness. For shoes, put on the peace that comes from the Good News so that you will be fully prepared. In addition to all of these, hold up the shield of faith to stop the fiery arrows of the devil. Put on salvation as your helmet, and take the sword of the Spirit, which is the word of God.

Let's break down our daily wardrobe.

BELT OF TRUTH

Paul says the first thing you should put on is the belt of truth. At first, I found a belt a rather odd item to be of such importance. It's usually the last thing you put on after you get dressed. But then I realized I was picturing the wrong type of belt, like those flimsy little straps the hosts make you wear on *What Not to Wear* to "create a waistline." This is not that kind of belt. It's like one of those champion rodeo belts with the huge buckles. You know, the metal ones that say "Cowboy Up" in huge letters and go halfway around your body. The kind that could probably deflect a bullet. But *our* spiritual belt is made of God's solid truth.

In John 8:44, Jesus called Satan "the father of lies." The best way to destroy lies is with the straight-up truth. When the Enemy comes after us with lies about our value or our self-worth, our belt of truth—God's truth—keeps us safe. It centers us and protects us with undeniable facts of God's goodness.

BODY ARMOR OF GOD'S RIGHTEOUSNESS

After we've got on our epic belt of truth (which, by the way, should've totally been the name of a 1980s hair band), we must protect our heart. It's time for the body armor.

Spiritually, hearts are delicate things. They can get broken easily. Satan desperately wants to convince you that you aren't worthy of being loved. He wants to shatter your heart and make you believe all your past sins have made you unlovable.

Nothing could be further from the truth. You *are* worthy of being loved. And you're righteous, not by your own doing, but through Christ's blood, which covers you and makes you worthy. Second Corinthians 5:21 says, "For God made Christ, who never sinned, to be the offering for our sin, so that we could be made right with God through Christ." It's *His* righteousness, not your own, that protects you.

Believing in Christ's sovereignty can fully protect our hearts from attack.

SHOES OF PEACE

Have you ever gone on a trip and discovered that you're wearing uncomfortable shoes? You can't return home to exchange them for better ones, so you're stuck with them for the remainder of the trip. With every step, raw blisters irritate your feet. You stop and take off your shoes whenever possible, but every step is pain.

Spiritually, when you don't walk grounded in the comfort of God's peace, your whole life can be filled with strife and pain. Constantly fighting for your own will decimates your tranquility and makes you vulnerable to attacks from the Enemy.

Instead of walking through your day with the mind-set of *I have to make things work out my way*, try starting your day by believing this: *God has me exactly where He wants me for today*. Choose His peace instead of your own forced will. You'll find your walk smoother.

SHIELD OF FAITH

Wouldn't it be nice if there was a way to stop Satan before you ended up taking a direct blow to the body? Well, there is—with the amazing shield of faith! (Sorry if I sound like a Ronco infomercial, but in all honesty, the shield of faith *is* rather nifty.)

By choosing to believe that God is always good and always in control, our faith can form a shield around us that no fiery arrow can penetrate. Satan is just looking for an opening to flick a small, burning ember of doubt inside us that says God isn't for us after all. All it takes is a little spark turning into a blaze to totally consume our relationship with God. By placing our trust in His goodness, however, that arrow of doubt will just bounce off our shield like an armadillo on a trampoline.

HELMET OF SALVATION

Now it's time to protect our brains. This is always a good idea, whether we're evading zombies or taking a mental pummeling from Satan. (The latter *is* the more severe of the two predicaments.)

When we put on the helmet of salvation, we put on the belief that we're forever God's protected children. This isn't just an insignificant, passing belief, like, *I look good in hats.* No, it's a wrap-around-your-head, glued-to-your-very-self-image belief, the kind that can't be shaken from your mind no matter how many lies Satan screams into your ears.

SWORD OF THE SPIRIT

Last, Paul implores us to take up the sword of the Spirit. This is the only weapon listed in our daily armor; all the other items are defensive gear. Our armor is all we need most of the time during spiritual attacks. If we have the truth protecting our minds and hearts, we can let the strikes bounce right off us. Sometimes, though, we're called to fight back—not with our own strength alone, because our human resources just aren't enough in a spiritual battle, but by relying on God's Word.

Hebrews 4:12 describes God's Word as "alive and powerful" and "sharper than the sharpest two-edged sword." Our own human-made devices—arguing, quarreling, chastising—are likely to have little effect against a spiritual attack. God's truth, on the other hand, can slice through any spiritual nonsense. To have that weapon at the ready, you must have it close by. Don't leave your greatest weapon for spiritual warfare—your Bible—on a bookshelf, collecting dust. Put God's truth in your hands, your mind, and your heart. Read it. Devour it. Know it.

For cosplayers, dressing up in elaborate garb at conventions and contests is a fun hobby. It gives them a break from reality and lets them use their whimsical imaginations and skills for a playful pursuit. For Christians, however, daily dress-up is vitally important to our spiritual walk. We're in a battle for our hearts and minds, and our spiritual armor should be the first thing we put on every morning.

Even before our Spider-Man underwear.

3

IDOLS

STAR TREK:
THE ORIGINAL SERIES

Dear children, keep away from anything that
might take God's place in your hearts.

1 JOHN 5:21

You are wholly *un*qualified to write a chapter about *Star Trek*," said my sister when she learned I was writing this book.

"*Sput!*" I sputtered. "Am too!"

"You can't name a *Star Trek* episode within the first five minutes of the show. I can."

She was right. I cannot. She can.

"Fine, I'll let you pick the episode," I said.

"Agreed."

Here's the episode my Trekkie sister chose.

The 1960s science fiction television series *Star Trek* follows the space adventures of the crew of the starship USS *Enterprise*. The series takes place in the twenty-third century, in the Milky Way galaxy. A confident and brash Captain James T. Kirk is the ship's commander, and their mission is primarily exploring new worlds and seeking out new life-forms. Interestingly, many of those new worlds look like the southern

California desert, and life-forms look like humans with body paint. But maybe that's how it is in the twenty-third century.

Episode 15 in Season 2, "The Trouble with Tribbles," begins as Captain Kirk and his crew arrive at Deep Space Station K7 to respond to a distress call from a Federation agricultural official. While there, the crew takes a bit of rest and relaxation while Captain Kirk and Mr. Spock deal with a Federation secretary who's concerned about transporting compartments of grain. Kirk and Spock assure him they will protect the shipment. Meanwhile, at the bar, a communications officer named Lt. Nyota Uhura meets a trader, Cyrano, who's trying to sell his wares to the local bartender. He also has a pet tribble for sale, a chirping ball of fluff. The sweet creature delights Lt. Uhura, so Cyrano gives it to her. She takes it back to the docked *Enterprise* to cuddle.

The tribble is adorable, but there's a problem: Their species is born pregnant, and soon Uhura's one tribble becomes two, then three, and then a whole lot more.

At first, the crew members are enthralled with the fluffy creatures. Lt. Uhura gives them away to anyone who wants to adopt one. But soon they're *everywhere*: the medical bay, the transporter room, all over Kirk's command center. All the crew members are struggling to do their jobs. The tribbles are eating all the food aboard the *Enterprise* and entering the ship's air ducts. They get into the Federation's grain shipment. Mr. Spock even notes that the tribbles are consuming their supplies and returning nothing.

The tribbles, who once seemed small and sweet and harmless, are now an enormous problem.

The same is true for idols.

* * *

Today's idols don't look like they did in Old Testament times. They aren't huge golden calves in the middle of the desert. Instead, they can look like bright-red sports cars, diplomas from Ivy League universities, or even a body well chiseled from hours spent at the gym. No matter what they look like, though, idols are just as much a problem today as they were when Moses had to do some serious golden cow tipping in the book of Exodus.

I had an idol problem a while back. Like the tribbles, my problem started harmless enough, and even with the best intentions. Before I knew it, though, my idol crept up on me and began taking over my life.

My idol was scrapbooking.

I've always liked taking photographs. Before the dawn of digital cameras, people were limited to how much film they could afford to buy for their 35mm cameras. Back then, most people bought the 24-exposure roll of film—or maybe the 36-exposure roll if they had a holiday coming up. Then they posed their friends and family and pets and snapped away. They had the film developed, glanced through the photos, threw out the blurry ones, and then shoved the rest into a small, plastic, pocketed photo album. Occasionally, they'd pull out the album to prove to a friend how bad their hair looked last St. Patrick's Day.

At least that's what I did.

Then one day at a friend's house—I remember the moment very clearly—she asked me if I wanted to look at the scrapbook she was making. *Scrapbook? What? Didn't teenagers do that in the '50s?* I thought. She opened a mammoth, pink, fabric-covered album. My jaw dropped. It was an album of photos spanning her daughter's life so far, yet it was nothing like I'd ever seen before. Every page was a bedazzled work of art: multicolored photo captions. Charms. Stickers. *Fuzzy* stickers.

I specifically remember thinking how good that wonderful scrapbook made my friend's life look. Never mind that her kid was currently sitting next to the scrapbook, shrieking and covered in spaghetti. In the scrapbook, life looked so lovely, sorta like an old-school Instagram feed. I wanted to get me some of that.

I started my scrapbooking hobby with small intentions. My first scrapbook was about my cat, Nouwen. He had recently spit one of his baby kitten teeth into my hand, and I thought, *Well, that should be preserved for posterity.* I got a small scrapbook, a few kitty stickers, and a cute little cat tooth envelope, and, suddenly, there I was: a woman who makes cat scrapbooks.

In the next years, I made a few more scrapbooks with old vacation and camp photos. I got a few more supplies too: edging shears, hole-punching thingies, special glue, and double-sided tape. This was something I did for fun just on the weekends.

Then I had myself a baby, and things quickly got out of control.

Around this time I also got a fancy-schmancy digital camera with fast shutter speed and a zoom lens. That camera made every photo look fabulous, and it accurately captured how positively adorable my daughter was. Every single photo was a treasure to me. I couldn't even bring myself to delete any of the multiple photos I'd taken of the same baby pose or baby burp or baby crawl. To me, each photo represented a moment in her life I could never get back, and it seemed imperative that I preserve them all.

Man, did I ever take a lot of photos. *Thousands.* And because I felt compelled to document each photo in a meaningful way, my scrapbooking went into overdrive. I bought every pink baby sticker, pink baby border, and pink baby paper I could lay my hands on. I got a huge carrying cart for all my supplies. I even went on a scrapbooking retreat, where I won the award for the most scrapbook pages completed in one weekend.

Every time my daughter napped, I was in the living room, documenting her life like a mad woman. Each scrapbook had so many photos that it could document only a few months of her life. Then I had to move on to the next one.

One night we got a tornado warning. My crazy scrapbooks were so important to me that I loaded them into the bathtub, where we sat on them until the alert was over. No way were my precious baby books going to fly away in the whirling wind if I could help it. But if they were, then phooey, I was flying away with them.

One afternoon I heard my daughter calling me from her crib, awake from her nap. I was irritated, because now I had to stop working on my scrapbook. When I got her out of her crib, though, she just wanted to be rocked until she fully woke up, and as we rocked, my irritation faded. I held her and smelled her hair, and I just wanted to stay with her like that forever, in that single moment.

Suddenly it dawned on me that my incessant scrapbooking was a big problem.

I thought about why my scrapbooking had become such an obsession, and I think it was this: When my daughter was born, my love for her felt big and scary. I had never felt anything like it. I mean, before I had a child, I figured, sure, I'll have all those expected motherly feelings and think my kid is swell. But then I got knocked over by this tidal wave of love I never saw coming.

I wanted to save every single precious moment and treasure it, but time kept slipping away from me. Deep down, I think I felt that, by meticulously scrapbooking every moment of her life, I could freeze those moments forever, make them look perfect, and own them. But really, I was just trying to control something I wasn't meant to control. I was meant to appreciate the gift and give thanks.

I had let scrapbooking become an idol in my life. Instead of worshipping God and being thankful that He had given me such a precious gift—this child—I was desperately trying to create cheap paper shrines.

Idols can overtake you like that. They can seem innocent and fluffy and chirp at you like a tribble, but *anything* can become an idol if you let it—your career, your retirement fund, your spouse, your Instagram account, your dog. As soon as you start depending on a substitute for the role only God should serve in your life, or you start worshipping one of His gifts rather than Him, you have an idol.

God *really* detests idols. The Bible is filled, front to back, with warnings against them:

So, my dear friends, flee from the worship of idols.
1 CORINTHIANS 10:14

You must not have any other god but me.
EXODUS 20:3

Those who worship false gods turn their
backs on all God's mercies.
JONAH 2:8

I get God's anger. We are His children, and He's fiercely protective of His role as our Father. Can you imagine how furious you would be if your child, whom you love and adore, started treating a ham sandwich or a toaster oven or a dirty sock as if it was you? Giving it good-night kisses? Spending every minute of the day with it instead of with you? Calling it Daddy or Mommy? It sounds ridiculous, but that's essentially what you're doing when you worship something other than God.

Sometimes, you just have to sit down, take stock of your life, and ask yourself a hard question:

There's nothing inherently wrong with posting hazy-filtered selfies online...

...but is it my god?

There's nothing inherently wrong with rescuing stray animals...

...but is it my god?

There's nothing inherently wrong with [insert object here]...

...but is it my god?

If you answer *yes*, you have an idol problem, and you need to swiftly deal with it. But how do you do that?

ASK GOD FOR FORGIVENESS

First things first: You need to tell God you're sorry. Thankfully, we have a loving, merciful Father. He's eager to forgive you when you go to Him with a repentant spirit.

GET HELP, IF NEEDED

Some of our idols are clingy little suckers. If your idol is an addiction to substances or pornography or food, you might need outside help to get untangled. In addition to asking God for help, reach out to support groups or counselors who have lots of experience with those addictions.

GET RID OF IT

Last, when you find yourself with an idol problem, you might take a cue from the way the *Star Trek* crew got rid of their tribbles. They loaded up all those creatures and teleported them onto a Klingon spaceship. BAM! Immediate expulsion.

If you struggle with worshipping an idol, you probably need to eject it from your presence entirely. It's hard to focus on God when you have an idol hanging around in your home, your phone, or your computer. Get rid of it.

I gave up scrapbooking. I stopped taking multitudes of photos. I let go of all the patterned paper and fuzzy stickers and stencils. I gave away the wheeled organizing cart. I got it all out of my house.

I didn't, however, jettison my completed scrapbooks. I figure they might mean something to my daughter someday, so they sit on a high shelf in her closet, collecting dust. I don't get confused about their importance anymore, though. They are nice remnants of memories, but they aren't important in the eternal scheme of things. They aren't my god.

If you have an idol—adorable and harmless as it might seem—get real with yourself. Ask yourself the tough questions. Worship the real God, not a worthless knockoff.

4

DECEPTION

WALLACE AND GROMIT

Stay alert! Watch out for your great enemy,
the devil. He prowls around like a roaring
lion, looking for someone to devour.

1 PETER 5:8

W hen I was in college, the art department at the smallish Texas
university I attended had only three art professors for the many
art courses I took. I'm not sure how it works with art professors in general, but mine were all quirky. Talented, brilliant, and passionate, but quirky.

One of them seemed to have *no* interest in traditional teaching.
His name was Bob. He didn't like being referred to as a professor, and
he preferred to think of his classes as "hanging out together." He also
didn't like us to create art during class. Bob thought it was more important for us to chat about life. That was all well and good, but I really
needed to learn some color theory.

One of his favorite class-time activities was digging through the
library's media center archives. He'd saunter into class and announce
something like, "*Cirque Du Soleil!*" Then off we'd trudge as a class to
find old VHS Canadian circus tapes to watch in some dusty audio-
visual room in the depths of the library.

One day he announced, "*Wallace and Gromit!*" I had no clue what he was talking about, and I thought he'd finally lost his mind. But then he introduced me to the wonderful world of British claymation, which turned out to be far more fun and life-enhancing than learning about art composition (of which I still know squat). So I thank you, dear Bob, for your unusual teaching methods.

The *Wallace and Gromit* series is the creation of Nick Park of Aardman Studios, a British production company that specializes in claymation (or to be more exact, *plasticine*mation, because the characters aren't actually clay). Each frame of a typical Aardman production is painstakingly crafted by hand. Through the years, the Aardman animators have built a cinematic world of pirates, sheep, chickens, and other delightful characters. *Wallace and Gromit* is one of their most beloved creations, telling the adventures of an absentminded, cheese-loving inventor, Wallace, and his long-suffering dog, Gromit.

In the *Wallace and Gromit* short "The Wrong Trousers," we find our two heroes enjoying breakfast and celebrating Gromit's birthday. Wallace has bought Gromit a new collar, a new leash, and a pair of mechanical trousers to take him out for his daily "walkies." (Gromit isn't that impressed with these gifts.) The two soon realize Wallace has spent the last of their money on the presents, and Wallace proposes that they rent out their spare bedroom to pay their bills.

A new renter arrives, and Wallace is happy to have found a fix to their problem. Gromit, however, takes one look at the chap and becomes suspicious. Something about him is vaguely sinister. Something is not to be trusted. Something about those beady eyes is disturbing. And he's also a penguin. Gromit keeps a sharp lookout.

Soon Gromit notices that the penguin has taken an extra-keen interest in the mechanical trousers. While Gromit grows even more wary of the lodger, Wallace is wooed into friendship with him, sharing tea and kinship. Distraught, Gromit decides to leave home, allowing the evil penguin to spring into action. He retrofits the mechanical trousers to be remote controlled, and then he devises a secret plot to use Wallace and the trousers to rob a local museum of a huge diamond.

Thankfully, Gromit remains vigilant. While following the penguin and observing his diabolical plan, Gromit realizes their renter is Feathers McGraw, a wanted criminal.

When Feathers completes his robbery, returns home, and traps Wallace, Gromit takes matters into his own hands. To stop Feathers from fleeing with the stolen diamond, he bravely faces off with the deceitful bird in a final, high-drama toy train chase. Finally, with Wallace's bumbling help, Gromit manages to capture Feathers and transport him to jail. Wallace and Gromit happily collect their reward money and dispose of the mechanical trousers, while Feathers languishes in his zoo jail cell, where he belongs. Wallace and Gromit celebrate with cheese and crackers (of course).

• • •

Gromit's battle with a duplicitous penguin might seem off the wall, but battles with deception are a daily occurrence in our lives. We must always be on guard.

Gromit showed himself to be a wise companion, on the watch for deception. Early on, he saw through to Feathers McGraw's true nature, which Wallace failed to do. Sometimes we're more like Wallace. We don't remain as vigilant against trickery as Gromit was, and the results can be devastating. This can happen to anyone who's caught unaware, even chosen women and men of God.

One such example comes from a story in the book of Judges. In the time before kings ruled Israel, God appointed judges to give leadership and wisdom to His people. And boy, did they ever need it. The Hebrew people were constantly forgetting about God and worshipping false gods and idols in their new land. Repeatedly, God was forced to put His special people into spiritual time-outs, letting them be ruled by oppressive foreign nations until they came back to their senses. Yet God still loved them, and He sent them those specific people called judges to help get them back in line.

Samson was born during one of these harsh times. The Israelites had once again returned to their corrupt ways, so God allowed the Philistines to rule them for 40 years. During that time, a man and his wife from the Israelite tribe of Dan were struggling with infertility. An angel appeared to the wife and told her she was about to become pregnant, but he also had some instructions: no drinking wine or beer, no eating certain foods, and no cutting their baby's hair. They agreed to them, and Samson was born.

His parents fulfilled God's requirements, and Samson grew up big and mighty, although a bit headstrong. Well, more than a bit. He was *very* headstrong. Samson loved God and was blessed by Him, but he also did what he wanted, when he wanted. Sometimes what he wanted was a fling with a prostitute or killing a Philistine. His character makes him a rather complicated biblical hero, but for the rough time the Israelites were currently living in, they needed a strong personality like Samson.

The Philistines hated him and were constantly looking for ways to destroy him. Over and over, Samson defeated and humiliated the Philistines. He gave them riddles they could not solve, burned their houses to the ground, and slaughtered great masses of them. Try as they might, the Philistines could not seem to defeat Samson.

They didn't know the secret to his strength was his uncut hair.

Then came ol' Delilah.

After years of making trouble for the Philistines, Samson fell in love with a woman named Delilah. The Philistines took notice of their relationship and cut a deal with her. If she seduced Samson and learned the source of his great strength so they could subdue him, she'd get a big payout. She agreed to try.

First, Delilah flirtatiously asked Samson, "Aw, honey, please tell me the source of your strength." Samson told her he'd be weak if he were tied up with seven bowstrings. Delilah waited until Samson fell asleep and tied him up with seven bowstrings. After he woke up, he easily snapped the cords.

At this point in the relationship, it would be fair to assume that Samson would be wise to no longer trust Delilah, correct? Maybe he should have ditched the woman who tied him up with bowstrings even though he'd *specifically* told her that would make him weak. But Samson didn't clue in. He went back for more day after day, and day after day Delilah begged for his secret. He always gave her a fake answer, and *every* time Samson found himself bound up in the exact manner that he said was his weakness. Did he think this was just a coincidence?

Somehow Samson couldn't seem to put two and two together, though: The love of his life was out to get him.

Finally, Delilah pulled out the big guns: the *L* word. She pouted and nagged and implored, "Listen here, Samson, how can you say you love me and refuse to tell me the truth? Why won't you tell me the secret of your strength?" *Wah wah wah.* (Imagine the music here from a tiny, sad violin.) Samson gave in and told her his secret: If his hair were cut, he'd lose his strength.

Well, of course, Delilah promptly let the Philistines in after Samson fell asleep, and they cut off his hair. When he woke up and tried to fight back, Samson found he had lost all of his strength. The Philistines gouged out his eyes and threw him into prison.

Samson had spent his *entire* life—literally since birth—in a battle against the Philistines, and he was deeply devoted to God and to using his might against his enemies. So it would be easy to write off Samson as stupid for trusting Delilah when she was so obviously up to no good. But when you sit back and think about it, it took some masterful trickery for him to throw it all away. That woman had some serious skills—manipulation, love bombing, and feigning innocence—and Samson fell for them.

Deception can ensnare *anyone* if they aren't staying alert to what's happening.

Being taken in by deception can also have long-lasting consequences, leaving you broken, alone, confused, and questioning what the truth really is. Unrecognized deception can send you down a path of ruin and destruction, just like it did for Samson.

It helps to know what forms deception can take so you can be wary. In Colossians 2:8, Paul says, "Don't let anyone capture you with empty philosophies and high-sounding nonsense that come from human thinking and from the spiritual powers of this world, rather than from Christ."

Yes, deception comes in many forms—more than Feathers McGraw's wooing or Delilah's seductions.

LIES

The most obvious form of deception is straight-up lying. Lying can create huge walls between people because it destroys trust. It stinks to have to learn this lesson, but not everyone tells the truth. If someone in your life has lied to you often, be on your guard. That person will most likely lie to you again.

FLATTERY

Flatterers use buttery words they don't mean to get something they want. It can be easy to be taken in by the wooing of flattery, but those words are a facade. Nothing is behind them—no trust, no honesty, not a real relationship. Getting taken by flattery leads to disappointment.

FALSE PROMISES

When someone purposefully misleads you with no intent to deliver, that's a false promise. By knowingly manipulating facts and crafting a rosy view of the future, some people will tell you anything to get what they want. They'll often promise riches, ideal health, or even "a better way to God." God wants us to be wise, but also patient, because He'll expose the truth in His own time.

HYPOCRISY

Hypocrites are experts at portraying themselves as living one way and yet living another life entirely. They preach actions that they themselves have no intention of taking. If you tie yourself to hypocrisy, you'll eventually find yourself with your own integrity on the line.

SELF-DECEPTION

This is the most dangerous kind of deceit. When you deceive yourself, you're pulling the wool over your *own* eyes. You can do this by:

LISTENING TO GOD'S WORD WITHOUT ACTING ON IT

James 1:22 says, "Don't just listen to God's word. You must do what it says. Otherwise, you are only fooling yourselves."

NOT HAVING A REALISTIC VIEW OF YOURSELF

Paul wrote to the Romans, "Because of the privilege and authority God has given me, I give each of you this warning: Don't think you are better than you really are. Be honest in your evaluation of yourselves, measuring yourselves by the faith God has given us" (Romans 12:3).

CONSIDERING YOURSELF PERFECT, WITH NO NEED OF JESUS'S REDEMPTION

First John 1:8 tells us, "If we claim we have no sin, we are only fooling ourselves and not living in the truth."

I find it a bit ironic that by *not* metaphorically opening his eyes to Delilah's tricks, Samson physically lost them. We don't have to be blind to what's really going on. We can ask God to open our eyes to the danger that's near, like Gromit's eyes were open when faced with Feathers McGraw.

You can fight against all forms of deception with truth and courage. Be on your guard.

5

MENTORSHIP
MEN IN BLACK

You have heard me teach things that have been confirmed by many reliable witnesses. Now teach these truths to other trustworthy people who will be able to pass them on to others.

2 TIMOTHY 2:2

I've always envied the closets of cartoon characters like Charlie Brown or the Simpsons. I love that they get to wear the same thing every single day. I hate making decisions, and I would be perfectly content to choose from a row of identical outfits every morning.

I'm not too far from getting there, though, because most of my wardrobe is black. The reason has less to do with any desire to be dark and brooding than it has to do with laziness. With a predominantly black wardrobe, most stains don't show, and everything matches.

I'd probably make a good mime.

Or a modern dancer.

Or a secret governmental alien crime-fighting agent.

Whichever.

Men in Black is the story of James Edwards III, an NYPD police officer recruited into a secret government agency. James is a good cop, quick on his feet and with a sharp mind. After chasing down a strange, lizard-eyed perpetrator on the streets of the city, he catches the attention of a mysterious agent known only as Agent K.

K's agency is looking for a new recruit, and he asks James to apply. During an extensive interview process, James shows K he can think creatively, make wise decisions, and act independently. K is impressed with the young candidate, and James is chosen to join the Men in Black.

Soon he learns the truth about his new employer's purpose: to monitor the presence of alien life-forms on earth. James thinks long and hard about his decision to join, but in the end, he chooses to commit to the organization even though that means he has to leave his former identity and life behind. He is assigned the name J, and K takes J under his wing.

K immediately must deal with J's immaturity and bravado. At first, J chafes under the tutelage of K. He doesn't like the car they drive. He doesn't like the tiny energy weapon he's been given. And he thinks his own usual methods of chasing down bad guys will get the job done. But he soon learns policing aliens is quite different from policing humans. Several times his impulsivity causes havoc, both at headquarters and in the field. Time after time, K respectfully but firmly corrects J, and then keeps training him.

Soon the agents are faced with a menacing threat to earth: an alien called a "bug." This body-snatching creature is looking for a power source in the form of a micro galaxy, so his race can wage war. The disgusting beast causes destruction wherever it goes. As the bug creates more and more wreckage, K and J scramble to protect the unsuspecting planet. The very existence of earth is on thin ice if K and J don't come through.

Little by little, J realizes the older and wiser K knows a thing or two about fighting aliens, and that his guidance is spot on.

If only J will heed it…

• • •

Building a mentoring connection can be a challenge.

Mentoring is more than on-the-job training or leadership. It's a relationship, requiring both the mentor and the mentee be equally engaged in the process. If either one shirks their part, the relationship won't work. But if both parties are willing to trust and invest in the other, the results can be life changing.

The book of Ruth tells the story of one such mentoring relationship.

Back when judges governed the Hebrew people, a famine occurred, and a man from Bethlehem in Judah decided to move his wife and two sons to Moab (present-day Jordan). Later the man died, and his wife, Naomi, was cared for by her two sons, who then married two women, Orpah and Ruth. They all lived in Moab together for a long time, but then the sons died, leaving the women without a man to care for them. Back then women had a tough time caring for themselves because of how society was set up.

Naomi decided the best thing was to pack up and head back to Bethlehem, trusting that God would take care of them there. The three women set out for Judah, but then Naomi implored Orpah and Ruth to go back to Moab and find new husbands. Orpah, despite loving Naomi dearly, headed back. Ruth, however, would have none of that. She said to Naomi,

> Don't ask me to leave you and turn back. Wherever you go, I will go; wherever you live, I will live. Your people will be my people, and your God will be my God. Wherever you die, I will die, and there I will be buried. May the LORD punish me severely if I allow anything but death to separate us! (Ruth 1:16-17).

Yes, Ruth was in it with Naomi for the long haul.

It must have been scary and overwhelming to be Ruth once they got there. She had left behind her native country, trusting that Naomi (and, more importantly, God) was leading her to a better life. But not only was she now homeless; she was a foreigner. Her only support and guidance came from Naomi, a poverty-stricken widow who couldn't offer much in the way of protection or financial security.

Once they got to Bethlehem, Naomi and Ruth had to support themselves. It was the beginning of the barley harvest, and Ruth decided to glean the fields—a potentially risky business. She would be picking up scraps the harvesters left behind, which might mean a day full of hot and exhausting work only to end up with very little grain, depending on the crop. The harvesters might also be jerks and chase her away. Worse, as a woman alone in a field in the middle of nowhere, she would be vulnerable to sexual predators.

But God looked after Ruth and put her exactly where she needed to be. She began gleaning in a field owned by a kind man named Boaz, who had compassion for this woman who was a stranger to him. He noticed she'd been working steadily in his field for hours, so he inquired about her. He was told Ruth was the young woman from Moab who had come back with her mother-in-law, whom she treated so well.

Boaz approached Ruth and told her, "Just stay in my field and glean. Hang out with my harvesters. I've told my people not to harass you. In fact, drink out of my water buckets if you're thirsty." Later, Boaz invited her to join his workers at lunchtime, giving her food to eat. Then he ordered his workers to leave some good barley specifically for Ruth to glean.

Ruth was overwhelmed by Boaz's kindness. She went home to tell Naomi about her day (and to give her the leftovers from her lunch). Naomi was astonished by the amount of grain Ruth had gleaned. She asked who had taken such good care of her, and Ruth told her the man was named Boaz.

Naomi was delighted, and she revealed that Boaz was a close relative, someone known as their "kinsmen redeemer." If he chose to do so, Boaz could seek the right to purchase Naomi's deceased husband's land and take care of all his former responsibilities, including his family. Naomi advised Ruth to stay close to Boaz's fields until the harvesting season was over, which she did.

When harvesting season was nearing its end, Naomi pulled Ruth aside and told her, "I want you to have a good life and a good home. I think Boaz is the answer for you. But you need to make a move to let him know you want to be his wife." She advised Ruth to get herself cleaned up, put on perfume, and go to the barley threshing room floor. After Boaz fell asleep, Naomi said, Ruth should chastely lie at his feet to hint that she was available for marriage.

Ruth took Naomi's advice and followed her plan to get Boaz's attention. When Boaz woke up, he was startled—but thrilled—that she was lying at his feet. Ruth brought up the prospect of marriage, and Boaz jumped at the idea. In the early morning, Ruth returned to Naomi, who reassured her that Boaz was a good guy and that he would make a wedding happen. Ruth didn't need to be impatient or go overboard and make a fool of herself by flirting. She just needed to wait.

Sure enough, the next morning Boaz set out to finagle the details of his marriage to Ruth. He obtained the right to buy the land, also receiving the right to marry Ruth in the process.

Boaz married Ruth, and they had a son, making Naomi a proud, doting grandma. They all had a new family to love, a family whose members became ancestors to Jesus Christ.

The story of Naomi and Ruth might have turned out quite differently if either woman had chosen to look out only for her own interests. There might not have been such a happy ending…

> …if Naomi had not included Ruth in her plan to pursue a better life in Bethlehem.

> …if Ruth had not remained loyal to Naomi along the journey.

> …if Ruth had not gone out to glean to help feed their little family.

> …if Naomi had not advised Ruth to chastely get Boaz's attention.

> …if Ruth had not taken Naomi's advice to wait patiently for Boaz.

Naomi and Ruth were there for each other. Each step along the way, Naomi poured her wisdom and love into Ruth. Ruth, in turn, listened to and embraced her mother-in-law's guidance. Because of this devotion, they made a terrific team.

A mentorship can be a powerful tool for change and growth in a mentee's life. Throughout history, God has placed people together to bring about growth: Moses and Joshua, Eli and Samuel, Elijah and Elisha. Jesus Himself mentored 12 disciples, who would in turn spread the gospel "to the ends of the earth" (Acts 1:8).

What does it take to be a mentor? Formal theological scholarship? Extensive mentoring workshops? Years of experience? None of these things. Many people are scared off by the idea of becoming a mentor because they think perfection is required. But the only requirement is leading with love. A mentor only needs to be a few steps ahead of a mentee and willing to invest the necessary time and energy.

The makings of a good mentor are simple:

Encouragement

...building up someone's confidence and hope

Listening

... just sitting and letting someone pour out their heart

Gentle guiding

... offering sound advice while not insisting on their way or the highway

Availability

... showing up and being dependable

Of course, this coin has a flip side. A mentee must also choose to share, listen, and heed the wisdom offered. A lot of us aren't quite as compliant as Ruth was. We're more like Agent J in *Men in Black*. We want to be show-offs. We want to talk more than we listen. If we hear sound advice we don't like, we ignore it and do our own thing. But many of us finally wise up and begin to learn humility.

Agent J eventually catches on. During the final showdown with the bug, he makes a wise choice. He lets go of his headstrong bravado and trusts that Agent K knows what he's doing, even as crazy as the situation is. J watches as K lets himself get eaten by the enormous alien so that K can battle it from the inside. Then when J shuts down his own fears, choosing to do the job K has been training him to do all along, they defeat the bug together.

Earth is saved because two people united—mentor and mentee.

What kind of mentorship might you need in your life?

6

BLINDSIDED
THE PRINCESS BRIDE

> Stay alert! Watch out for your great enemy,
> the devil. He prowls around like a roaring
> lion, looking for someone to devour.
>
> **1 PETER 5:8**

Here's a fun fact about me: I'm scared to death of rats and snakes swimming up through my toilet.[1]

Some people may wonder where their weird phobias come from. Well, I can tell you *exactly* where my phobia came from. When I was a kid, I was watching an episode of *Highway to Heaven*. Michael the angel got a job as a plumber, and there was a toilet snake problem. "This is a *thing*?" a horrified eight-year-old Ellen shrieked. "Why was I not told this was a *thing*?" Apparently it is, and I've been checking toilets ever since.

It certainly doesn't help that every six months or so, some terrible, horrible, no good, very bad friend sends me a news clip of a toilet snake or toilet rat from somewhere in the world.

Nothing about a toilet rat scenario pleases me.

But that's nothing compared to the rodent problem Buttercup had to deal with when she entered the Fire Swamp in *The Princess Bride*.

In this fairy-tale adventure, Buttercup—a beautiful yet simple

---

1. I'm assuming this is the first devotional in history to mention toilet rats.

country girl—falls in love with a poor farm boy, Westley. Despite their pure and devoted love for each other, Westley heads out to seek his fortune so they can get married. His ship is attacked at sea by the Dread Pirate Roberts, and Buttercup is informed of her beloved's death. Her heart is broken.

Years pass, and Buttercup has essentially given up on life. Still, her beauty attracts the attention of the region's prince. She doesn't love him, but she agrees to marry him, having nothing else to live for anyway. Then days before the wedding, Buttercup is kidnapped by a band of henchmen. Little does Buttercup know they've been hired by Prince Humperdinck to start a war with a neighboring kingdom.

Before long, the henchmen notice they're being closely followed by a mysterious man in black. Using their strengths—swordplay, brawn, intellect—they attempt to thwart his advances. He manages to overcome each one until, at last, he's left alone with a very ticked-off Buttercup. Believing her rescuer to be her love's killer, she pushes him down a steep hill.

As he falls, Buttercup realizes he is, in fact, her sweet Westley. She throws herself down the hill after him. After they're passionately reunited, they find themselves pursued by the prince and his men. Westley and Buttercup dart into the infamous Fire Swamp to escape.

The Fire Swamp is a hot mess—literally. It's a jumble of vines, infernos, and creepy crawlies, which Westley and Buttercup are forced to gingerly navigate. Luckily, the prince's men want nothing to do with the Fire Swamp, so the duo is safe. Well, not really "safe." Safe-*ish*.

As Westley and Buttercup make their way through the treacherous maze of terrors, it's easy for them to be distracted. They have just been reunited after many long years, and they're eager to catch up. They want to make goo-goo eyes at each other, but the Fire Swamp is not exactly a place where they can let down their guard.

Each time they turn their attention to each other, they're blindsided by a Fire Swamp hazard and must act immediately. First, Buttercup is almost engulfed in the flames of a flame spurt. Westley quickly smothers the fire on the skirt of her dress, and they cautiously continue along their path. For their next pitfall, Buttercup falls into a pit of lightning sand, and down she goes. Westley grabs a vine and dives in after her. After an uncomfortably long time, he drags her out, and they both gasp for air.

This is not going well.

Just as Westley assures Buttercup they've got it all under control, they encounter their biggest threat yet: an enormous R.O.U.S.— Rodent of Unusual Size. As Buttercup looks on in horror, Westley is brutally attacked by a nasty, human-size rat. He wrestles it away as best he can, but the rodent's sharp teeth bite into his arm. When the rat starts heading for his beloved Buttercup, Westley springs into action. He's badly hurt when the R.O.U.S. bites into his shoulder, but it meets a gruesome demise, by his sword.[2]

By the end of their Fire Swamp detour, Westley and Buttercup are beaten up but still alive. Feeling victorious, they limp out of the swamp—and are blindsided once again by the prince's waiting troops.

• • •

We can also get blindsided if we aren't careful. It can happen quite easily, even to those of us who should know better.

Eli was the high priest at Shiloh, the location of a major Israelite worship temple. One day Hannah, a woman who struggled with infertility, visited the temple during her family's yearly pilgrimage. Overcome with despair, she sobbed and prayed to God for a son, vowing, "I will give him back to you. He will be yours for his entire lifetime, and as a sign that he has been dedicated to the LORD, his hair will never be cut" (1 Samuel 1:11). Eli noticed her, assumed she was drunk, and scolded her. (Heads up, gentlemen. When we women are upset, don't always assume we are drunk.) Embarrassed, Hannah explained that she was in deep pain and was asking God to help her.

Eli's heart softened. He saw her distress and prayed that God would give her what she asked for.

God heard Hannah and Eli's prayers. Hannah's son, Samuel, was

---

2. It would be the same in my household, but probably with a toilet plunger.

born the next year. As soon as she was finished breastfeeding him, she brought him back to Eli. This act was a huge sacrifice on Hannah's part. Eli took Samuel in and taught him how to be a priest. Eli was devoted to serving the Lord, and he guided Samuel to do the same.

One night young Samuel was repeatedly awakened by a voice calling his name. Each time, he wandered into Eli's room and asked him what he needed. Eli kept sending him back to his own bed—until he realized *God* was speaking to Samuel. Wisely, he instructed Samuel to stop and listen. Samuel obeyed, and that encounter sparked a lifelong relationship with God.

Because of Eli's guidance, Samuel learned to listen to God. He also became a major force in shaping the nation of Israel.

As well-meaning as Eli was, though, he had a tremendous problem lurking in his life. Rather, he had *two* problems: his own two sons.

Hophni and Phinehas served with their father as priests at the temple in Shiloh. First Samuel 2:12-13 says, "The sons of Eli were scoundrels who had no respect for the LORD or for their duties as priests." When people brought their animal sacrifices, the sons had a servant stick a fork in the pot while the meat was boiling and give them whatever meat came up with the fork. Sometimes Hophni and Phinehas had their servants take the meat before it had even been burned at the altar. The Lord detested them for stealing His offerings. What's more, they were having sex with the women who served at the temple entrance.

Eli's sons were the nasty R.O.U.S.es of his life. While Eli was busy tending to his priestly duties and teaching Samuel, his sons were creeping in the background, taking a huge chomp out of the holiness in the temple. This filthy business went on for years.

Eventually, Eli heard rumors about his sons' behavior and scolded them. Hophni and Phinehas needed to be expelled from the temple and held accountable for their actions, which only Eli had the clout to do. But he didn't do it. He only scolded them, and when they didn't stop their vile activities, Eli even benefited from them.

That was a big mistake. A man came to Eli with a message from the Lord: Not only would his inaction lead to *everybody* in his family dying young, but the few descendants still permitted to serve at God's altar would be allowed to do so only so their hearts would break to see their children die a violent death. Then he was told Hophni and Phinehas would die on the same day to prove what God said would come true.

Sure enough, when Samuel was older, a terrible battle occurred between the Israelites and Philistines. The Ark of God was stolen, and many Israelites were killed, including Hophni and Phinehas. When Eli learned the ark was gone and that his sons were dead, he fell off his seat and died as the result of a broken neck. And that was the end of Eli.

Honestly, that's a sad end for a man who was probably a decent enough fellow. But decent or not, Eli didn't do what needed to be done when sin crept in and blindsided him.

As Christians, sometimes we're fixated on staying clear of certain "well-publicized" sins. We pick and choose which sins are "the bad ones"—maybe stuff like murder and adultery and cockfighting—and as long as we stay away from those, we feel pretty good about ourselves. We feel proud and complacent. But before we know it, other sins can creep into our lives—sins a little more covert or "acceptable" within today's church. Maybe sins like:

- racism
- pride
- viewing pornography
- worshipping wealth
- bitterness
- prejudice against outsiders

These sins can devour our souls like lightning sand—and we never see them coming.

What we choose to *do* about sin makes the difference. Rather than looking the other way, like Eli did, we must fight against it. As soon as we see the sin manifest in our lives, we've got to beat the snot out of it, like Westley and Buttercup beat the R.O.U.S.

How do you fight back?

- *Ask God to show you if you have a sneaky sin problem.* Just ask Him. He'll show you, quite plainly. Sometimes you might not really want to know, but you can be brave. Ask.

- *Turn your sin over to God and ask forgiveness.* Our God is full of goodness and mercy. Ask for His forgiveness and for Him to give you a fresh start. He'll hear you.

- *Keep fighting back.* Don't let your sin keep coming back for more. Reach out for extra help, if you need to—like an accountability partner, so you have a buddy to help you fight. Don't let sin win.

Westley and Buttercup made it through many more trials—torture, death, and a fake marriage—before they eventually got their happily ever after. They kept their eyes open to new threats, and they fought back to the very end.

You can fight too. Just keep your eyes open so you're not blindsided. Especially by a toilet rat.

7

APPEARANCES
EDWARD SCISSORHANDS

> The LORD doesn't see things the way you see them. People judge by outward appearance, but the LORD looks at the heart.
>
> **1 SAMUEL 16:7**

I have no idea what happened to my hair genes. One of my sisters has beautiful hair with Botticelli-like curls. My other sister has ever-so-subtle, yet lovely, beachy waves. And then there's my hair: frizz. Rebellious curls. Strands of gray starting in college. It's unfair and obnoxious.

Every morning, I look in the mirror and talk to my hair.

"Look here, Hair," I say. "You don't like me, and I don't like you. But let's do this thing."

Then my hair shakes its insolent fist at me, and we begin our daily power struggle.

On the days I feel as if I have a fighting chance, I use oil, heat, and violence to straighten the tar out of my hair. It pouts, but it stays down. Before long, though, it resumes its insubordination. Usually, I just give up and let my hair be its funky self, and then people ask me all day if I'm feeling well.

I know I shouldn't care. This world is full of more serious problems than hair rebellion. But I think it's a universal habit to fret about outer beauty to some extent. As much as we hate to admit it, the world judges by appearances.

They certainly judged poor Edward Scissorhands.

Edward Scissorhands, a movie created by Tim Burton, is a unique fairy tale about a misunderstood outcast and his attempts to fit in with a rainbow-pastel, cookie-cutter suburban community.

Edward, a kind and gentle soul, is the creation of his inventor "father" in a Gothic mansion laboratory. Before completing his work, the eccentric man passes away, leaving Edward with scissor blades as hands and very little knowledge of the scary outside world. Edward continues living a lonely existence in his hilltop mansion until a compassionate Avon lady named Peg comes calling. She immediately decides to take sweet Edward home with her.

At first, Peg's traditional family is admittedly distrustful of the misfit Edward. He could not look more different than the rest of the community. He's pale, nervous, and covered in cuts from his blades—quite different from the resident soccer moms, jocks, and cheerleaders with perky hair and matching pastel outfits.

Edward tries his best to fit in. He learns he's most accepted for his helpfulness and unique skills: sculpting topiaries, grooming dogs, and styling elaborate hair creations. But before long and because of their envy and spite, members of the community manipulate Edward's naïveté. They tire of his usefulness and begin to use his innocence against him.

Kim's mean-spirited boyfriend, Jim, instigates a situation where Edward appears to be a thieving danger to the community. The rest of the community shuns him.

Peg's daughter, Kim, however, slowly begins to understand the beauty within Edward. He is kind. He is honest. He is brilliantly creative. Despite the community's judgment, as she dances under the snow among his beautiful ice sculptures, she sees his pure heart.

Jim, however, is overcome with jealousy and anger at the growing bond between the two. Through a series of unfortunate events, Jim convinces the community that Edward and his scissorhands are a terrible danger to others. Edward is misunderstood, scared, and brokenhearted.

Edward flees to his secluded mansion atop the hill. Kim chases after him, followed by a vengeful Jim.

Jim attacks Edward, but Edward doesn't fight back. As Kim attempts to intervene, Jim slaps her, and Edward snaps. Trying to defend Kim, Edward regrettably stabs her jealous ex, and Jim falls out of a window to his death.

Kim and Edward both realize Edward is better off in his secluded hideaway than at home with her because he'll never be accepted for who he is. She kisses him and leaves, grabbing his spare scissorhands on her way out of the mansion. Showing the scissorhands to the townsfolk, she tells them both Jim and Edward are dead. She forever misses Edward, but she remembers him whenever it snows.

◆ ◆ ◆

It would have been nice if Edward's neighbors could have seen past his awkward appearance to appreciate his gentle spirit. But the truth is, our real-life pettiness isn't much different. Our world worships thigh gaps, chiseled chins, and svelte bodies—certainly *not* sharp shears attached to appendages.

Sometimes it takes God's pointing out the truth for us to see what's important.

Samuel the priest was nearing the end of his life. His two sons should have been preparing to take over his Israelite management duties after he died, but they were turning out to be corrupt dolts. Israel didn't want their leadership. The elders got together and demanded that Samuel appoint a king for Israel.

Samuel knew that was a terrible idea, but he prayed to God about the request.

Now, since the beginning, God had given Israel plenty of appointed leaders: Moses, Joshua, and a handful of judges and priests, deeming them sufficient for His people. God wanted the nation of Israel to be set apart from all other nations. So what if every other nation had a ruler? Israel was not every nation. They were God's chosen people. Over and over, God tried to drill into their heads that they were called to a different standard than the rest of the world. They were to look different, behave differently, think differently, and worship differently. Israel didn't need an earthly king; they just needed *Him*.

But the people still clamored for a king.

Someone with charisma.

Someone with a commanding presence.

Someone to make Israel look legit.

Finally, God decided to give His people what they wanted—a king. Of course, God already knew how bad this would turn out. He knew kings send people to war, force them into hard labor, and take resources for their own selfish use. But God must have seen the need to let His people figure out—the hard way—that He knows best.

One day not too long afterward, God gave Samuel the heads-up that he was about to meet the future king of Israel. Samuel was on the lookout, and sure enough, there he was: Saul.

Saul had it all going for him. He was young, handsome, strong, and heads taller than most men. (I bet his hair smelled good too.) He looked every bit the part of a king. Samuel took Saul out to lunch and revealed that the young man was chosen to be the new king of Israel.

When Samuel made his announcement to the nation, the people were ecstatic. They finally had what they wanted: a tall, good-looking ruler of Israel.

At first, Saul seemed to relish his new role, and he followed the rules God specified. He led his soldiers to victory against many neighboring territories, and although he did have some obedience slipups, he generally listened to Samuel's advice.

Then God commanded Saul to destroy the neighboring Amalekites, a nation that hated and continually attacked Israel. And when God said, "Destroy," He meant it. Like, every last thing, from their king to their pet goldfish. Total annihilation. He was clear on that.

But Saul didn't obey Him. Instead, he decided to capture the Amalekite king and keep some of the good cattle and sheep. Granted, he burned the livestock as an offering to God, making his disobedience okay in his mind, but that's not what God told him to do.

God instantly regretted making Saul king (see 1 Samuel 15:10-11).

God could see that, at his core, Saul was not the leader He wanted for His people. Saul's outsides may have been gorgeous, but his insides were selfish and disobedient. Saul wanted glory for himself, not God.

He warned Samuel that He was going to take the kingdom from Saul and give it to someone after His own heart. God sent Samuel to stealthily meet with Jesse, a man from Bethlehem with many sons.

When Samuel first arrived at Jesse's house, he took one look at his oldest son and thought, *Yes! That's him! The new king!* (Maybe his hair smelled good too.)

But the Lord said to Samuel, "Don't judge by his appearance or height, for I have rejected him. The LORD doesn't see things the way you see them. People judge by outward appearance, but the LORD looks at the heart" (1 Samuel 16:7).

The next son was presented. And the next. And the next. Seven sons altogether. But each one was a big, fat NO. Finally, Samuel asked Jesse if he had any sons left. Jesse told him he had one more—the youngest, a shepherd boy out in the field. Samuel immediately sent for him.

When David arrived at the house, God told Samuel, "This is the one; anoint him" (1 Samuel 16:12).

Yep, that's right. Little David. He wasn't a bad-looking kid, yet he certainly wasn't the ideal picture of a great nation's king. But God didn't care what David looked like. He saw his heart, and it was sweet, loyal, and good.

Samuel anointed David and prepared him to take over as king.

It's a relief to know that God doesn't give a hoot about our outward appearance. If He did, most of us would be up the creek without a paddle. None of us is a specimen of human perfection. We've got weird moles, sweaty armpits, excess earwax, and cellulite. Some scissorhanded folks might even be out there.[1]

Not only that, but the reality is that everything around us—except our soul—is in a constant state of decay.

---

1. I'm guessing in Brooklyn.

OUR BEAUTY DOES NOT LAST

Charm is deceptive, and beauty does not last; but a
woman who fears the LORD will be greatly praised.
PROVERBS 31:30

Physical beauty is fleeting. Even for the few supermodels who exist, glamor eventually fades and new supermodels take their place. Standards of beauty even change from year to year, and it's impossible to keep up. Some days, beauty means a spiral perm; other days, it's long, slinky hair. You just can't count on outward beauty.

OUR CIRCUMSTANCES AND SURROUNDINGS
ARE CONSTANTLY CHANGING

The grass withers and the flowers fade, but
the word of our God stands forever.
ISAIAH 40:8

You never know what life will bring. Your big, beautiful house might burn down to the ground tomorrow. All of your trendy wardrobe will probably be out of style in a month or so. Your hair might fall out. Life is perpetually changing. Our only constant is God.

OUR BODIES ARE AGING

That is why we never give up. Though our bodies are
dying, our spirits are being renewed every day.
2 CORINTHIANS 4:16

You can stick to a meticulous regimen of exercise, sunscreen use, and organic food consumption. You can pump your body with all sorts of plastics and fillers and dyes. You can tuck this thing up here and staple that thing down there. But age catches up with all of us eventually. At some point, we're all going to sag and bag and drag.

God knows that worrying about outward appearance is futile. He wants us to pay attention to the beauty of our souls—the soul being what's going to stick around for eternity—rather than obsess about our looks. A truly beautiful soul comes from the refinement of loving and spending time with God. He loves seeing a pure heart fully focused on Him.

Stop fretting about your outsides! God loves your insides more than you could ever know.

8

COURAGE
SUPERHEROES

> So be strong and courageous! Do not be afraid and do not panic before them. For the LORD your God will personally go ahead of you. He will neither fail you nor abandon you.
>
> **DEUTERONOMY 31:6**

I think about superpowers a lot. Like, a *lot*. Like, probably too much to be socially acceptable.

Waiting in the grocery line…thinking about superpowers.

Brushing teeth…thinking about superpowers.

Watching a superhero movie in a theater…surprisingly, *not* thinking about superpowers. I'm usually thinking about getting more butter for my popcorn and some Junior Mints.

I've questioned the origins of my superpower obsession, and the only genesis story I can come up with is the Underoos craze of my youth. My love affair with my Wonder Woman underwear might have set me up for a slight, lifelong superhero fixation.

One hang-up I have with superpowers is that all the good ones are taken: strength, invisibility, Spidey senses, flying, healing, and running kinda fast. It's not fair, hogging all the superpowers like that. Which ones are left?

I don't know. Fruit?

"Tangerine Woman and Her Eye-Blinding Tanginess?"

Doubtful that Marvel is gonna come knocking on my door for that one.

Recently, I was pondering superpowers as I was traipsing through the woods—

Hold up, there. The previous statement sounds as though I'm some sort of outdoor enthusiast, prone to taking long, thoughtful walks in the wilderness. *Oh, there goes Appalachian Ellen. Packing up her latest state-of-the-art mountain gear, setting out to ponder the meaning of life, off the grid in the woods...*

No.

I was just chaperoning my daughter's overnight field trip at a remote nature center, and the fact that I was even there proves the sheer love I have for her, as opposed to any love I might have for muddy, ant-covered elements. The outdoors and I have a complicated relationship. I appreciate it *in theory*, but too much out there wants to bite me, fall on me, slip out from under me, hunt me, lick me, poison me, and scab me. I generally leave the indoors only when forced.

Or for the people I love. Hence, the field trip.

The day we hiked through the mountains, rain poured for hours. Here I was prancing around outdoors, and it wasn't even good nature. It was *wet* nature. Slopping through the mud and dirty leaves and snakes, I wasn't the picture of loving, maternal sacrifice. I don't like being wet and cold and muddy. I was grumbly. I even whined to my daughter's teacher, "What about an overnight in an art museum? Where was the sign-up for that one?"

As I was slogging through the caves and steep, muddy trails, I thought to myself, *It sure would be nice to just transport myself back to the lodge.*

I started fantasizing about all the possible ways I could use super-powers to get out of my current, distasteful situation.

Flying above the mountains...back to the lodge.

Taking big strides with giant, elastic legs...back to the lodge.

Using superstrong tree-breaking force...*back to the lodge.*

As my brain slowly slipped back into reality, I happened to look down at the little girl walking directly in front of me on the trail. I realized she was struggling, and I studied her.

She walked with a limp—because of spina bifida, I believe—and she often had to grasp nearby trees to keep from losing her balance on the slippery rocks. Sometimes she grabbed onto her patient friend in front of her. She was also so focused on climbing the trail that she probably hadn't noticed her poncho had slipped halfway off her shoulders. She was soaking wet, caked in mud, out of breath…

Yet smiling.

Well, huh.

While I'd been grumpily daydreaming about becoming a superhero to avoid discomfort, I had missed the pint-size hero who was limping along right in front of me.

The truth is that comic and movie superheroes aren't the perfect picture of courage. Yes, they go off into battle possessing extraordinary powers and strength. They can break down walls. They can haul the enemy off to jail, wrapped in spiderwebs. They can generate force fields of protection. They can easily do amazing feats and save the day. But is that true courage?

Not really.

True courage is getting up again when you've been knocked down a thousand times. It's repeatedly being told you're worthless, and then choosing not to believe it anymore. It's trying your best while knowing you'll most likely fail. It's fighting for good and justice when the bad guy seems so much bigger (and has way more power and money). It's saying, *Yes, Lord, I am willing*, despite being extraordinarily ordinary and deeply flawed.

Courage is a little girl struggling up a slick, muddy mountain trail. The thing is, real heroes generally don't look the way you'd expect.

* * *

David was one of those heroes. I'm not talking Older David in the Bible: David the Soldier, David the Leader, David the King. I'm talking about Younger David: David the Shepherd, David the Younger Brother, David the Kid.

At the time of David's youth, Saul was the king of Israel. The Israelites were at war with the Philistines and having a mighty hard time beating them. They were camped near the Valley of Elah, having reached an impasse. The Philistines had sent their largest warrior, Goliath. For what it was worth back then, he was their "superhero."

David, a young and smallish son of a local shepherd, had been sent by his father to the front lines to deliver food to his older brothers. When David arrived at the Israelite's camp, Saul and his men were terrified at the prospect of what they were facing. Nobody wanted to face off with the giant Goliath. But as little David settled in and got caught up on all the drama, he was like, "*Ffffft*. Whatever. We've got God on our side. If you guys are going to be weenies about it, I'll face Goliath myself."

Of course, Saul and his men were relieved that they weren't going to face the giant themselves. But they *still* didn't get it (God being on their side), so they plopped a bunch of Saul's armor on David. He told them he didn't want to wear it because he wasn't used to it, but I also think it probably made him look ridiculous and hardly able to move. I imagine he looked a bit like a Bugs Bunny medieval knight cartoon.

David was wiser than the army of men and shook free of the armor. He knew if he relied on his own power and strength against Goliath, he'd be a dead man. Instead, he reminded himself of the truth: God was in control.

David picked up a few stones and his slingshot and headed out to meet the giant.

When Goliath saw the small, ruddy-looking youth coming to battle him, he had a good laugh.

But then:

Plink.[1]

Thud.[2]

---

1. That's the sound of a stone hitting a forehead.

2. That's the sound of a Goliath hitting the ground.

As monstrous as Goliath was, he was no match for a small stone, David, and God.[3] As soon as Goliath was dead, David detached Goliath's head from his body, and the Israelites defeated the Philistines.

With God's help, David won the battle. But you know what? Sometimes you don't win. Sometimes, for God's own mysterious purposes and reasons, He allows the stone to miss the forehead. Sometimes you slip and land in the large mud puddle of life next to an angry snake. Sometimes you even know winning is highly unlikely, but you try anyway because you know God is on your side.

We may be small and facing tremendous obstacles, but God tells us to be strong and courageous. And not always winning is okay. You aren't a hero because you always win; you're a hero because you trust God—and you *try*.

When you head into the rough world, remember that you're already a hero when you try, no matter the possible outcome. God has your back...*and* your front...*and* all the parts in between. You're boxed in by His love and protection.

---

3. The key factor in this equation being God.

9

OVERWHELMED
TETRIS

When I am overwhelmed, you alone
know the way I should turn.

PSALM 142:3

hate packing for a trip.

I'm notorious for avoiding the packing process until the last minute. I'll get the bags out and put them in the middle of the floor and walk by them for a day or two. Occasionally, I'll halfheartedly throw in a bottle of travel shampoo or a pair of socks. It's almost as though I'm waiting for the Packing Cavalry to stroll in from off the streets and start packing my bags for me, but in my heart I know no cavalry is ever going to appear.

When I finally accept that I'm my own packing squadron, I frantically run around like a mad woman, throwing everything into those bags. There's no rhyme or reason, like toothbrushes wrapped in swimsuits. It's mayhem, but at least it's all finally in one place.

What I *really* hate about packing, though, is arranging bags in a car trunk. My tactic is to feign confusion and incompetence until someone who has high visual spatial intelligence pushes me out of the way to work their stacking talents. I love watching someone who intuitively knows where the items should go.

I guess I should just spend more time on my Tetris.

Tetris is simple enough. It's the nice little computer game where you stack squares in straight lines. Geometric tiles, in the form of four blocks each, descend from the top of the playing screen. As the shapes fall, the player can manipulate the objects' positions to create a horizontal row of tiles at the bottom. If the row of tiles has no gaps, the whole row disappears.

Tetris has a dark side too. That's when the game stops messing around and picks up speed.

As the game progresses, the tiles start falling progressively faster. You have less and less time to manipulate the objects before they hit the bottom, and soon the rows start stacking up higher and higher. Before long, you become overwhelmed by the sheer number of tiles raining down on you and the buildup of poorly constructed bottom rows. Tiles soon engulf you, and it's GAME OVER.

Sometimes you can feel like the world is crashing down on you, faster and faster. You're doing all you can to keep up, but it's no use. You're about to be buried.

I think we all go through those overwhelming times. I certainly lived through a time like that when I was dealing with infertility.

• • •

I always wanted to have a family, but I never thought this feat would become one of my biggest life challenges.

Honestly, I didn't think about having kids too much when I was younger. I was busy living my life, and I assumed that when I wanted a baby, I'd just go ahead and have a baby. It would just happen because that seemed to be the way it worked. As my friends began entering the baby-having phase of life and I started going to lots of baby showers, the notion became more real to me.

One day I was visiting my friend Shelley, who had recently given birth to a cute little nugget with a full head of dark hair. As I was holding the baby, I leaned over to breathe in that baby scent from her baby's head. Oh my goodness gracious. Such a glorious smell! What are those baby heads made of, anyway? Unicorn belly button lint? Someone needs to bottle that up and sell it.

I was hooked. I decided it was baby time for me. I researched a bit and decided I had it all figured out. I even picked out the month I wanted to get pregnant.

But it didn't happen.

Another month went by, and it still didn't happen. And another and another and another.

Something was wrong.

I remember Googling the word *infertility* for the first time. I was horrified to discover a whole infertile realm out there. It doesn't always "just happen." I suddenly found myself learning about endometriosis and basal temperatures and hostile womb environments. My head was swimming with my newfound label: *infertile*. No, no, no. This was decidedly *not* what I had planned.

I remembered all those women in the Bible who struggled with infertility: Sarah, Hannah, Elizabeth. I'd read their sad, desperate stories when I was younger, but I didn't expect to be in their barren sisterhood. But here I was: just one of the gang.

Well, I tend to throw myself into new projects wholeheartedly, and solving my infertility was no different. I was going to beat it. I began trying every fertility regimen I could find: charting, temperature taking, ovulation testers, standing on my head, hormone treatments, drinking green tea. Eventually, my battle progressed to fertility drugs, laparoscopic surgery, and medical procedures. Sometimes I felt like I was losing my mind with this twisty and turny balancing act.

Every month, I tried to line up all my little Tetris-like fertility blocks in perfect, orderly shapes that would result in a baby. And every month I was left with it all crashing down again—the confusion, the anger, the sadness—just like the month before.

I was utterly overwhelmed.

Infertility can make you feel like you are inferior to the rest of womankind. It's easy to start seeing your body as defective. It can also be tough not to wonder if God has forgotten about you or at least skipped over you in line.

Every day was a reminder of the empty spot where a child should be. It's not like you can permanently get away from babies, children, and families. Other women aren't going to stop getting pregnant and having babies just because you can't. You're still going to be invited to baby showers and baptisms and birthday parties. You can try to hide from the reminders of what you so desperately want, but that's a lonely existence. Everywhere you turn, you can feel like pain is raining down on you, and that pain can begin to consume you.

Feeling overwhelmed is certainly not limited to infertility. It can come from myriad other burdens:

- a heavy workload
- a crushing debt
- caring for aging parents
- poor choices made by loved ones
- a chronic illness
- the extra demands of parenting a child with special needs

Unfortunately, that's life.

I had a teacher who used to say, "Take it easy. And if you get it easy, take it twice." As an adult, I truly appreciate the sentiment, because it's so rare in life that we *do* get it easy. Life happens, and with it comes intense burdens we never saw coming.

But thankfully, we have some steps we can take if we find ourselves overwhelmed by life's troubles.

SHIFT YOUR FOCUS BACK TO GOD

You will keep in perfect peace all who trust in
you, all whose thoughts are fixed on you!
ISAIAH 26:3

When you're under stress and living with worry, it's easy to focus on your own small world. But God wants us to stop and look at Him.

Our problems may seem huge and towering, but God is bigger. He can handle anything we place in His mighty hands.

LET HIS CALM AND PEACE OVERTAKE YOU

I have told you all this so that you may have peace in me. Here on earth you will have many trials and sorrows. But take heart, because I have overcome the world.

JOHN 16:33

After you get your focus back on God, you probably need a rest from the situation that was burdening you. Pause. Breathe. Take it easy. Then take it twice.

Just sit with God's peace for a while.

TAKE THE NEXT STEP GOD PUTS IN FRONT OF YOU

When I am overwhelmed, you alone know the way I should turn.

PSALM 142:3

It's easy to be overwhelmed when so much seems to be coming at you at once. But you're not meant to deal with all of it at the same time. Don't do anything until God shows you the next right step.

LOOK TO HIM FOR RESCUE

The Lord hears his people when they call to him for help. He rescues them from all their troubles. The Lord is close to the brokenhearted; he rescues those whose spirits are crushed.

PSALM 34:17-19

God not only rescues us in various ways, but His rescues often aren't what we're expecting.

My real rescue from infertility came in the form of building a closer relationship with God. I wanted a baby, but God knew what I really needed was *Him*. It took me a long time to realize that, though. I was so consumed with overcoming my troubles on my own that it took a while for me to see He was using my burden to show me how to rely on His love and peace. His rescue was more focused on growing my faith than on giving me children. I certainly wouldn't wish the pain of infertility on anyone, but for me, it became a blessing.

My family-building story has a happy ending. After my initial battle with infertility, God miraculously blessed me with the pregnancy that gave me my daughter. Then after she was born, I assumed the ache for children would finally leave my heart—but it didn't. If anything, it was worse.

I couldn't get over a nagging heartache telling me someone was missing. I found myself dealing with secondary infertility, which for some reason was much longer and even more painful than the first time around. But I was right. Someone *was* missing: my son, who arrived through adoption (a miraculous story as well).

My path to parenthood wasn't the way I planned to welcome children, but I can't imagine my kids coming any other way.

10

CONSEQUENCES

SUPERMAN

Don't be misled—you cannot mock the justice
of God. You will always harvest what you plant.

GALATIANS 6:7

uspension of disbelief is a necessary requirement to be a proper geek. If anyone's written a *Handbook for Geeks* out there somewhere,[1] it probably has a full chapter on how to string your disbelief on a clothesline like a pair of wet socks. To embrace our beloved sci-fi and fantasy worlds, we geeks have to turn off our inner-reality editor.

We don't question when a mud bath makes the hero invisible to the alien.

We shrug and say, "Well, okay" when the protagonist and villain switch faces and hop around on high-speed boats.

We nod along when children are shrunk with a laser rather than, you know, blasted into a million pieces.

Embracing our imagination is the geek way of life. But on the flip side of the coin, when you push a geek just a bit too far into disbelief, there's going to be some fit throwing.

---

1. My guess is that the official geek handbook probably looks a lot like *The Hitchhiker's Guide to the Galaxy* with "DON'T PANIC" written in bold on the cover. And it's most likely covered in orange Cheeto dust.

I remember my first baby-geek temper tantrum quite clearly. It was the early 1980s—before the VCR and cable television were popular sources of home entertainment. Back then, if you wanted to see a repeat of your favorite blockbuster film, you had to wait until one of the three major television networks cut you a break. About once a year, ABC or NBC or CBS would show a good movie—edited for content and time, of course—as a "Special Television Event." Usually around Easter, they played *The Ten Commandments* or *The Sound of Music*. Other standards were *Close Encounters of the Third Kind*, random James Bond flicks, and *The Wizard of Oz*. Christmastime brought multiple stop-motion specials, *A Charlie Brown Christmas*, and Dolly Madison Zingers commercials.

One time, when I was around six years old, I got to stay up late to watch the 1978 movie *Superman*. I was beyond excited.

Superman has all the makings of the perfect superhero origin story: An alien baby boy is sent to earth when his home planet, Krypton, is destroyed. Raised by loving adoptive parents, he begins his earth life in Kansas as Clark Kent—discovering his powers of superstrength, superspeed, supervision, superhearing (and, I'm speculating, super hair growth; I've often wondered how often Superman needs a trim). One day in his teen years, he unearths a mysterious piece of crystal in his barn. He leaves home and travels to the Arctic, where he uses the crystal to build his Fortress of Solitude. From a holographic recording made by his biological father, Jor-El, he learns all about his true identity.

Clark Kent eventually returns to human civilization, moves to the city of Metropolis, and lands a job as a reporter for the *Daily Planet*. There he meets a fellow newspaper reporter, the plucky and pretty Lois Lane. He swoons. She ignores him.

Lois's zest for reporting the news tends to lead her into trouble. Following a helicopter crash, Lois is left dangling from the side of the helicopter, high atop a skyscraper. Clark is called into action as his alter ego, Superman, to save her. He swoops in to catch Lois and the helicopter as they both fall. Clark may not have roused Lois's affections, but this Superman chap is another story entirely. Now it's Lois's turn to swoon.

Superman begins his superhero career to worldwide acclaim. He catches jewel thieves and bank robbers. He saves the president of the

United States from peril. He even rescues cats from trees. The ladies, especially Lois, are in love.

But Lex Luthor, an evil genius, has plans to get rich with a desert real estate scheme. Seeing Superman's newfound fame, Lex deduces that the superhero is going to be a problem for his nefarious plans. He plots to get rid of him.

With the help of his sidekicks, Otis and Eve, Lex lures Superman to his underground lair by threatening to gas Metropolis. Once Superman is there, Lex traps him with a shard of Kryptonite—the only substance to which the superhero is vulnerable. As Superman struggles, Lex reveals his plan: to fire two stolen government missiles. One will create a massive earthquake along the San Andreas Fault, causing California to fall into the ocean, making his desert-turned-oceanfront property worth millions. The other will head toward Hackensack, New Jersey, to cause a diversion.

Eve is startled to hear that Lex's plan includes a missile aimed at Hackensack, where her mother lives. After Lex leaves, Eve releases Superman from his Kryptonite death trap, on one condition: He must *first* stop the missile headed toward her mother in New Jersey.

Superman races away to save the world, and he keeps his promise. He stops the New Jersey missile by depositing it in outer space. Unfortunately, that meant neglecting the missile headed toward the San Andreas Fault—which his beloved, Lois Lane, happens to be near. The other missile detonates and triggers an earthquake.

Superman rushes to save Lois, but when he finds her lifeless body buried in rubble, he's overcome with grief and anger.

Superman flies into outer space and begins to fly around the earth at astronomical speed, counter to its natural spin. The planet begins to spin backward, turning time back as well. Superman returns to the very-much-alive Lois, and everything is hunky-dory again.

Up until the ending, my six-year-old self was totally on board. I loved Superman. He was *it* for me. Whatever he was selling, I was buying. But as I watched him rotate the earth backward to change the movie's ending, my suspension of disbelief crashed to the ground like a meteor in the middle of Siberia.

As the credits rolled, I sat there dumbfounded and thought, *Wait. What just happened?*

I may have been only a baby geek at the time, but I was not amused. If I had known what it meant back then, I would have been yelling, "Blasted *deus ex machina!*"[2] at the screen. But I was six, so I just yelled, "Poo!"

First, spinning the earth backward results in time reversal? No, sir. I don't *think* so. That's not one of the official time travel rules, and we all know it. I call foul, Superman.

Second, that ending is just *not fair.* You don't think we all want a rewind to delete our past mistakes? I mean, I have entire years' worth of junior high haircuts I'd like to erase out of existence.

Humph.

Unlike Superman, we don't get the opportunity to turn back time to undo mistakes and poor choices. We have to live with the consequences of our actions.

King David surely did.

* * *

When David was an established and powerful king, he made a big mistake. Well, he made a small *oops* that led to a transgression that led to a deplorable sin. The story takes place in 2 Samuel 11–12.

One day while standing on his roof, David saw Bathsheba, the wife of his solider Uriah, bathing. He was like, "Hubba, hubba." (Sorry, but that's the best way to put it without sounding creepy. Which it totally was. Really creepy.) David decided that, as the king, he should get want he wanted, and he wanted Bathsheba. David had Bathsheba brought to him and had an affair with her.

Lo and behold, she got pregnant.

Pretty darn soon David realized evidence of his sin was going to be a visible bump on Bathsheba's belly, a bump that could not have been

---

2. This is a plot device writers pull out of nowhere when they've written themselves into a corner. Whether the military, eagles, or the flu arrives to save the day in an unlikely fashion, that's *deus ex machina.*

put there by Uriah because he was currently away at war. David plotted his next move. He knew he had to act fast.

David had Uriah summoned home from the battle. He was hoping the man would sleep with Bathsheba and supposedly impregnate her, thereby covering up David's affair.

It was a sneaky little plan there—except that David didn't count on Uriah's loyalty to his troops. Uriah stayed in the palace barracks overnight with the other soldiers. David tried again the next night by getting Uriah drunk. Again, Uriah declined to stay with his wife.

David realized his current manipulative plan wasn't working, so he decided to try an even harsher approach. He commanded his captain to send Uriah to the front lines of battle and then pull back the forces to leave him exposed to the enemy. It worked. Uriah was killed.

David married Bathsheba, and she gave birth to a son. He really thought he had gotten away with it. But there's no "getting away with it" with God. God knew perfectly well what had happened, and He was ticked off.

Before too long, God sent His prophet Nathan to have a talk with David. Nathan sat David down and told him a story:

> There were two men in a certain town. One was rich, and one was poor. The rich man owned a great many sheep and cattle. The poor man owned nothing but one little lamb he had bought. He raised that little lamb, and it grew up with his children. It ate from the man's own plate and drank from his cup. He cuddled it in his arms like a baby daughter. One day a guest arrived at the home of the rich man. But instead of killing an animal from his own flock or herd, he took the poor man's lamb and killed it and prepared it for his guest (2 Samuel 12:1-4).

David was horrified by Nathan's story. In his heart, David was still a just person, but his sin had clouded his brain.

"That's awful!" he hollered. "This man deserves to die. What a selfish jerk. He needs to pay for his crime and lack of mercy!"

"Dude," said Nathan, "you are that man."

The truth hit David like a giant being knocked in the head by a rock. He felt horrible and immediately confessed his sin to God.

Nathan told David that God forgave him and wouldn't kill him, but he would suffer consequences for his actions: The infant son he'd had with Bathsheba would die. His wives would sleep with other men. Killing and murder would plague his family thereafter.

After Nathan left, David learned his infant son had fallen ill. David fasted and prayed and refused to eat. But as had been foretold, the child died. David also dealt with many years of rebellious, angry children— some of whom committed heinous sins against one another, like rape and murder. His personal family life was a mess.

It was a painful lesson for David to learn, and he dealt with the aftermath of his choices the rest of his life.

As much as we want to wipe our slate completely clean of errors, sometimes we're still left with life consequences. In Galatians 6:7-8, Paul says, "Don't be misled—you cannot mock the justice of God. You will always harvest what you plant. Those who live only to satisfy their own sinful nature will harvest decay and death from that sinful nature. But those who live to please the Spirit will harvest everlasting life from the Spirit."

Our actions have aftereffects we can't always shake. Sometimes our actions might leave us with a lifelong disease. Or jail time. Or the loss of a spouse. It can be hard to accept these long-term or permanent repercussions. But thankfully, God forgives.

David was certainly not the only biblical character to blow it big time. Lots and lots of people in the Bible were confronted with their sin. The difference with David is that he genuinely repented. So even though God was angry with David, and He let him suffer the consequences of his sin, He forgave him the moment David confessed and asked for forgiveness.

God can also return us to relationship with Him when we screw up. We just need to assume responsibility, confess, and ask for forgiveness. We can also ask God to show us where we went wrong so we won't make the same mistakes again.

Even though God doesn't always remove the consequences of sin, He can still bring beauty out of the rubble. Case in point: God eventually gave David and Bathsheba another son, Solomon, from whom Jesus descended. A rotten beginning still led to the birth of someone who would save the world. That's amazing.

God can use your mistakes to show His glory too.

11

DEPRESSION
DISNEY

He comforts us in all our troubles so that
we can comfort others. When they are
troubled, we will be able to give them
the same comfort God has given us.

2 CORINTHIANS 1:4

I have struggled with depression most of my life.

It's under control with medication, truth-seeking, and a whole lot of Jesus. But back when I was in college, depression was Roombaing all over my life. That means I just sort of lay there like a shaggy carpet while depression rolled over me and sucked all of the bits of joy and energy out of my body.

I fought back as hard as I could. I journaled. I prayed. I tried to will myself to be happy. But the dark cloud of depression followed me wherever I went.

That cloud was particularly bad the year I studied art in Florence, Italy.

It was actually embarrassing. There I was, in one of the most beautiful countries in the world, living in the center of Renaissance art and studying and practicing art, which I love. Everyone around me kept asking, *Isn't this amazing? Aren't you having the time of your life?* I desperately tried to find that enthusiasm. Instead, I felt ashamed that I was struggling with despair.

During breaks and weekends, most of the students at my school took train excursions to suck in as much Europe as possible. I, too, ended up wandering around Europe, staying in threadbare hostels, eating cheap street food, and sleeping in stinky overnight train cars.

Near the end of my school year, I still had some travel left on my Eurorail pass, so I decided to see Paris. By this time, faking the happy in front of others was utterly exhausting for me, so I took the trip alone.

Let me tell you, depression in the comfort of your own bed is tough enough. Depression while traveling alone is another beast entirely. Imagine constantly struggling to tell yourself that you are indeed a worthwhile human being who deserves to exist, all the while standing alone in the rain in Paris, watching 50 couples kiss in front of the Eiffel Tower. Several couples even asked me to take their photo. It would have been laughable except for, you know, the soul-wrenching agony.

While in Paris, I decided to take a day trip out of the city. Arriving at the train station one morning, I had two potential destinations. I could take a train to the Palace of Versailles, the extravagant seventeenth-century chateau of King Louis XIV. It was an educational excursion where I could roam the meticulously manicured gardens, visit the opulent Hall of Mirrors, and expand my mind with knowledge of the French Revolution.

Or I could take another train to Disneyland.

Of course, I went to Disneyland.

Euro Disney was relatively new at this point, and the French were still being snoots about visiting it. The park seemed nearly empty with just me and a bunch of Japanese and German tourists. I wandered around and rode various rides by myself all day. I ate whatever the French version of corn dogs happened to be.[1] I watched little children meeting their favorite Disney characters. I listened in on passing conversations, none of which were in English. I stayed in my own little, isolated world.

That afternoon it started to rain, so I looked for an inside ride to stay dry. Now, as I said, Europeans weren't particularly enamored with

---

1. *Le saucisse sur bâtonnet.* Basically, corn dogs wearing berets.

Euro Disney, but they were even less enamored with Disney's Mary Blair view of the world, featured in the ride "It's a Small World." It could have been called, "It's a Ghost Town": Ellen, virtually alone, riding through all the rooms full of happy singing dolls from around the world.

When the ride ended, nobody was waiting to take my place, so I just stayed on board. The French "Small World" ride attendant seemed to care very little about the wet, mousy, rule-breaking American girl. He let me sit in my little boat for an hour.

After a while, I began to cry. I was so worn out. I was so alone. I was so very sad.

That moment was one of my most miserable. Depression can be an ironic beast that way. It can engulf you even when you're in "the happiest place on earth."

I'm not the only person to struggle with depression. Even cranky Old Testament prophets endured that battle.

● ● ●

Elijah was a prophet of God who lived in a truly rough time in Israel's history, brutal for *anyone* who loved the living God and wanted to follow Him. There just weren't very many followers, and Elijah was the only prophet in all of Israel standing up for God. He was alone.

This was during the reign of King Ahab, who, according to Scripture, "did what was evil in the LORD's *sight*, even more than any of the kings before him" (1 Kings 16:30). Quite a legacy there. How would you like to be the one in the Bible with chapters and chapters devoted to how utterly awful you were? That was Ahab. Ahab was bad enough, but right out of the gate, he married the worst woman on the planet, Jezebel, daughter of the king of the Sidonians. You've heard people exaggerate and say, "Ugh, she's the worst" about someone? Well, in the case of Jezebel, it was true. She *was* the worst.

Ahab and Jezebel worshipped the fake god Baal, even going so far as building him a temple in Samaria. They also built a shrine to the sex goddess Asherah. They didn't just condone evil in their kingdom; they actively practiced it. What's worse, they led the whole nation of Israel into their pagan worship.

God was fuming that His people were once again being led away from Him. He sent Elijah to deliver several messages to King Ahab. First, to tell the king a drought was coming unless he changed his wicked ways. The king, of course, didn't change, and the people suffered without rain for three years. Elijah then returned to deal with Ahab again.

He asked that all 450 of the Baal prophets and 400 of the Asherah prophets be brought up to Mount Carmel. He also asked that all of Israel be present to witness the event. Once there, Elijah brought down the hammer. There would be a contest. The Baal prophets would offer a sacrifice to their fake god, and Elijah would do the same for the living God. Neither would light the altar themselves, but whichever "god" answered the offering with fire would prove to be the real God. Everyone agreed to the terms, and the contest began.

The Baal prophets hooted and hollered and tried every religious trick in their weird little book. Absolutely nothing happened. By noon, 450 blood-splattered Baal prophets looked ridiculous next to their ruined altar. Then Elijah stepped up to the plate. He created a new altar. And to make sure there would be no question about God's power, Elijah drenched the whole thing in water. He prayed to God, and immediately the offering was engulfed in flames.

Everyone was in awe and acknowledged that Elijah's God was the real God. Elijah ordered all of the fake prophets to be slaughtered. He also announced that God was ending the drought with a massive approaching thunderstorm.

Ahab reported everything that happened to Jezebel, and she was consumed with fury. She sent word to Elijah that she was going to kill him the same way he killed her fake prophets. Elijah was terrified, and he fled.

Elijah made his way to Beersheba in Judah, and then he walked another day's journey into the desert. There, he collapsed under the shade of a juniper tree. He was so completely depressed that he just gave up. "I have had enough, Lord," he said (1 Kings 19:4). He asked God to let him die.

Then he fell asleep.

But God doesn't forget us when we're at our lowest, and He didn't forget Elijah. He pulled Elijah out of his emotional pit, taking specific actions that demonstrate how He cares for us when we're depressed and discouraged.

GOD FED HIM

An angel woke Elijah, and then he told him to get up and eat. Beside Elijah was some bread and a jug of water. The angel kept encouraging Elijah to eat, giving him enough strength to continue onward to a cave at Mount Sinai.

Oftentimes with depression, just doing the basic stuff is exhausting. It's hard enough to climb out of bed, let alone eat and shower. Before we can confront our battle with depression, sometimes we just need to take baby steps and care for our primary needs.

A good way to figure out which step to take first is by practicing the acronym H.A.L.T. Ask yourself these questions:

Am I **H**ungry? Eat something.

Am I **A**ngry? Beat on a pillow.

Am I **L**onely? Call a friend.

Am I **T**ired? Take a nap.

Remember the gentle way God took care of Elijah and take care of yourself.

GOD SHOWED ELIJAH WHO HE IS

When Elijah was in a better physical state, it was time for God to show His glory. While Elijah was still in the cave, God asked him, "'What are you doing here, Elijah?' Elijah replied, 'I have zealously served the LORD God Almighty. But the people of Israel have broken their covenant with you, torn down your altars, and killed every one of your prophets. I am the only one left, and now they are trying to kill me, too'" (1 Kings 19:9-10).

Elijah felt despair. He had done everything in his power to stand up for the Lord, yet here he was, alone in a cave with a bounty on his head.

At that point, God chose to remind Elijah of His true nature. As Elijah stood on the mountain, the Lord passed by and a powerful windstorm hit. But God wasn't in the wind. Then came an earthquake, but God wasn't in that either. Then there was a roaring fire; again, not God. But then there was the sound of a gentle whisper, and *that* was God.

Sometimes when we're dealing with depression, we forget who God is. We become so wrapped up in our own despair that we can't see what's in front of our own noses. We can feel as though He isn't there—or at least as though if He is, He doesn't care much. That's why it's so important to remind ourselves daily that our God is desperately in love with us. He is, at His core, good and caring. He wants light for our lives, not darkness.

God also has His own way of solving problems. When we're struggling, we often want Him to roar in like a tornado and snatch away our distress. He might choose to work that way in some instances, but often He comes in like a soft, soothing whisper. We may want our depression to quickly blow away with a mighty gust of wind, but maybe God wants us to learn from it. Maybe a greater good is to be gained by enduring depression for a time, like learning compassion, learning to fight darkness, learning to reach toward truth. During these times, He wants us to reach out to Him, trust who He is, and find comfort in His presence.

GOD SENT ELIJAH A SUPPORT SYSTEM

After God showed Elijah who He is, He instructed him to go back to where he came from, anoint a new king, and prepare a man named Elisha to be a prophet of God as well. He also told Elijah that He was preparing 7,000 more people in Israel who would worship only the living God. Elijah wasn't alone after all.

Depression thrives in solitude. That's one of the trickiest aspects of depression. When you desperately need other people the most, depression makes you want to isolate. It convinces you that you're a burden and shouldn't bother anyone with your despair. During depression, one of the toughest actions is to reach out for help, but it's also the most necessary action.

God can send several different types of people to help you through depression. Sometimes it's an understanding friend. Sometimes it's a sister who orders you to wash your hair and take a walk. It might even be a doctor who can figure out if you need medication, or a therapist who can help you work on long-term issues and coping strategies. Whatever the case, you are not alone.

I'd like to tell you my day at "the happiest place on earth" ended in my having a breakthrough with my depression, and that I magically became "the happiest person on earth."

But I didn't.

I did, however, have a breakthrough with God. As I sat there on the ride, silently crying and praying, I felt a wash of comfort come over me. It was as if God was saying, *It's okay. I love you no matter what.* And I felt peace and love.

No, the depression didn't go away after that day. I've fought that obnoxious beast off and on for years. But I know, without a doubt, that God loves me and He's helping me fight it off. He's given me support systems, helped me learn mental tactics, and filled my mind with His loving truth.

Most importantly, He's helped me reach out to others who are struggling too.

12

DISCERNMENT
BILL AND TED'S EXCELLENT ADVENTURE

But test everything that is said.
Hold on to what is good.
1 THESSALONIANS 5:21

W hen I was a kid, I was delighted to no end when something wasn't as it appeared. Frankly, I usually found real life lacking, so I embraced any opportunity for whimsy and make-believe. I had a particular fondness for objects that were completely different on the inside than they were on the outside, such as...

Oscar the Grouch's trashcan:
Oh, YES.

Mary Poppins's bag:
Gimme.

Jeannie's bottle:
Sign me up.

Doctor Who's TARDIS:
Bring me one and I will marry you.

I've noticed that time machines especially seem to enjoy being masters of disguise. They have been known to hide on islands and in DeLorean cars, cosmic treadmills, hot tubs, and, of course, telephone booths. I have no idea why time machines are so into telephone booths. One would think time machines could travel into the future and see that telephone booths would soon cease to exist. But whatever. They still work for me.

It also worked for Bill and Ted, who discovered the benefits of one such fantastical telephone booth in *Bill and Ted's Excellent Adventure*.

Bill S. Preston, Esq., and Ted "Theodore" Logan III are teenage best friends, living in San Dimas, California. They're good-natured slackers who spend their days practicing mediocre music on their beat-up guitars for their garage band, Wyld Stallyns.

They're passionate about their music. But school? Not so much. The two have a history class report due, describing how historical figures would view modern-day life. Ted's police officer father threatens to send him off to military school if he flunks this class.

Little do Bill and Ted know how *crucial* it is that they pass this history class. The future of the world even depends on it. A future utopian society exists only because it was inspired by the music of the Wyld Stallyns. Therefore, they *must* pass the class. They *must* remain together as best friends. They *must* stick with their band. The leaders of the future society decide to take matters into their own hands.

As Bill and Ted attempt to piece together their history report while sitting at the Circle K gas station, the sky opens and a telephone booth lands right in front of them. A bearded man exits the booth and greets them. He announces that he's there to help them with their history report.

The boys are skeptical. But then another telephone booth lands nearby, and out walk the slightly futuristic versions of Bill and Ted. They implore present-day Bill and Ted to trust the man, whose name is Rufus. Present-day Bill and Ted are sold, and Rufus offers to show them how the telephone booth time machine works.

The boys come up with a plan. They begin to scout through time, picking up historical figures to help them finish their report. One by one, through a series of adventures, the boys bring home Napoleon, Billy the Kid, Socrates, Sigmund Freud, Joan of Arc, Ludwig van Beethoven, Abraham Lincoln, and Genghis Khan. They eventually end up in front of the Circle K again, urging their past selves to trust Rufus.

Bill and Ted drop off the historical posse at the local mall to experience modern life in San Dimas. After the crew causes a huge commotion, Ted's father arrests them. Bill and Ted need their new friends for their report, and they're running out of time. They wrestle with a solution, and, ultimately, they use their trusty time machine to plant key escape elements (like the jailhouse keys) around the police station.

Bill and Ted manage to help their new friends escape from jail, and everyone makes it to the school auditorium in time. Their report, presented as a rousing rock concert, is a huge success, and they pass their course. The future is saved!

The historical figures are returned to the past, and Bill and Ted get back to what they love—their band. As Rufus leaves Bill and Ted to return to his own time, he gifts the boys with brand-new electric guitars. After listening to them practice their horrible music, he assures the viewers that they'll get better—eventually.

Yes, that time machine telephone booth came in pretty handy.

• • •

As nice as it would be to have an everyday object with extraordinary powers, the reality is that none of us will ever own a phone booth that can travel through time and space. Or own a bottomless bag. Or own a wardrobe that leads to a vast, alternative reality. *Meh.* Sorry.

Another sobering truth is that people aren't always as they appear.

You start life full of trust. Trust that someone will feed you. Trust that somebody will catch you when you fall. Trust that you'll be told the truth. But it turns out that isn't always the way life works. Sometimes that person you trusted doesn't feed you when you're hungry. That person laughs at you when you fall. That person lies.

Some are forced to learn early that not everyone is trustworthy. This really stinks. As a young child, internalizing that people can't be trusted can bring its own lifelong baggage to unpack. Others learn trust lessons later, but eventually we all learn that liars and deceivers and cheaters bring pain.

It would be easy to navigate who is trustworthy if people's outsides matched their insides. But real-life monsters don't look like the Predator. Sometimes monsters just look like a smiling, elderly, next-door neighbor.

Deception is evil's primary mode of operation. Evil counts on us not being able to tell the difference between goodness and itself. If we could see the true grubby, twisted, sick nature of evil that lurks under the surface, we'd immediately run the other way. That's why it often presents itself as charming and attractive. It disguises its predator nature to look more like a cute Muppet. Evil doesn't play by the rules. The Bible says that Satan even disguises himself as an angel of light (2 Corinthians 11:14). That's a real scummy move, honestly. But then, it's Satan, and he's lousy.

Now, it's one thing to be deceived online by a fake Nigerian prince and lose some money. The real danger lies when we're deceived spiritually, when we're counting on people to guide us, or protect us, or even share a life with us, and they don't. Knowing whom to trust is vital to our spiritual health—and, frankly, to our entire life. Trusting or following or marrying monsters can end up killing us mentally, emotionally, spiritually, and sometimes even physically.

How can we look beyond mere appearances and tell what someone is really made of ?

We look at the fruit.

Have you ever walked into a downtrodden grocery store that has a distinct odor of rotting fruit coming from its produce section? We had a store like that in my town when I was growing up. If we ever had to go there to pick up an odd item our regular grocery store didn't have, we held our breath, got our jar of pickled oyster jam or whatever, and quickly checked out. I always wondered who on earth would choose to buy fruit there. Good fruit is amazing. Bad fruit is the pits.

In Matthew 7:15-20 we see that Jesus used the universal appeal of fruit to teach us about watching out for deceivers:

Beware of false prophets who come disguised as harmless sheep but are really vicious wolves. You can identify them by their fruit, that is, by the way they act. Can you pick grapes from thornbushes, or figs from thistles? A good tree produces good fruit, and a bad tree produces bad fruit. A good tree can't produce bad fruit, and a bad tree can't produce good fruit. So every tree that does not produce good fruit is chopped down and thrown into the fire. Yes, just as you can identify a tree by its fruit, so you can identify people by their actions.

The key word here is *actions*.

It's easy to get taken in by the wooing of words. Words can be pretty and alluring. They can make extravagant promises. They can point to riches, better choices, purity, and loyalty. But at the end of the day, words are just puffs of air if no action backs them up. First Thessalonians 5:21 says, "Test everything that is said. Hold on to what is good." If the actions aren't matching the words, there's a problem.

I'm one of those people who had a steep learning curve when it came to looking at actions, not just words. I'd find myself in a merry-go-round of heartbreak and hopefulness in certain relationships, mainly because I chose to believe empty promises and slick-sounding religious words rather than look at the reality of the other person's actions. Once I started looking at the fruit in their life, it became clear that I was expecting a rotten tree to produce good fruit. As long as I kept believing words and not actions, I was bound to keep feeling crazy and disappointed.

So what kinds of actions are we talking about? What actions should be a red flag? What actions should draw us in?

Paul summed it up nicely in Galatians 5:19-23:

> When you follow the desires of your sinful nature, the results are very clear: sexual immorality, impurity, lustful pleasures, idolatry, sorcery, hostility, quarreling, jealousy, outbursts of anger, selfish ambition, dissension, division, envy, drunkenness, wild parties, and other sins like these. Let me tell

you again, as I have before, that anyone living that sort of life will not inherit the Kingdom of God. But the Holy Spirit produces this kind of fruit in our lives: love, joy, peace, patience, kindness, goodness, faithfulness, gentleness, and self-control. There is no law against these things!

Satan tries hard to convince us that bad fruit smells good and looks appetizing. Heck, just turn on a standard television reality show and you'll see the full display of every kind of stinky produce: backstabbing, lust, immorality, violence, lying, and addiction. All that might make for dramatic viewing, but it's devastating to actual daily life. When you're ingesting bad fruit every day, you'll sicken your mind, your health, and your faith.

Choose instead to be involved with people who bring good things into your life: encouragement, hope, and love. They will build you up and point you to God instead of tearing you down and leading you to destruction. When your life is filled with goodness instead of rot, the difference is amazing.

Now, occasionally, you might find yourself in a situation where everything seems to be on the up-and-up. No red flags are waving. Words and actions seem to be matching up. The fruit currently appears to be okay. But there's still a small voice inside you screaming, "RUN!"

Listen to that voice. It's the Holy Spirit. Sometimes His command might not make much sense, but you just need to get out of there. The Holy Spirit knows what's lurking below the surface. He isn't fooled by appearances. You might find out later what the truth of the situation was, or you might not. But you can trust that the Holy Spirit has your best interests in mind. If He wants you out of a situation or away from a person, trust Him.

It can be difficult to discern the truth sometimes, especially when we truly want things to be good. As much as we want our telephone booth to be a time machine, sometimes when we open the doors we find it's just a telephone booth. Or worse yet, it's a telephone booth full of Texas cockroaches.[1] It's a cruel world out there, with many evil, nasty

---

1. Those monsters can *fly*.

things. Jesus knew this full well. In Matthew 10:16, He says, "'Look, I am sending you out as sheep among wolves. So be as shrewd as snakes and harmless as doves.'"

Thankfully, God didn't leave us without guidance. He gave us our excellent discerning brain and the Holy Spirit. Let's use those guides and trust Him.

13

GENERATIONS
GAMING

Remember your leaders who taught you the word of God. Think of all the good that has come from their lives, and follow the example of their faith.

HEBREWS 13:7

I've had game shame all my life.

I didn't grow up in a gaming household. My parents thought video games rotted the brain, so we had no Atari, no Nintendo, and no PlayStation in my house.[1] When we went to the pizza parlor, no quarters were given out for *Donkey Kong*.

The extent of my gaming experience came from a 1980s behemoth IBM computer and a few allowed educational games on floppy disks. I could learn to fly airplanes on *Chuck Yeager's Flight Simulator*. I could try to locate Carmen Sandiego. We had a math game where a squirrel hid nuts in a tree. All of the games were conquered by typing slow DOS commands like C:\ SUBTRACT FOUR ACORNS. No quick hand-eye coordination skills were practiced at my house as they were in most other homes in America.

---

1. My parents had a long list of things they thought rotted the brain. Among the other items: poor grammar, rap music, and artificial Christmas trees. They've since come around about the Christmas trees.

I developed an irrational fear of video games. When I visited friends' houses, I would grow uneasy when someone suggested that we play Nintendo. I had no idea how those controllers worked. I didn't know how to jump over turtles or why anyone would even need to do that. *Are the turtles good or bad? Do I want to gather the mushrooms? Or will they kill me? Wait. Why is the music speeding up?*

Why is the music speeding up?

WHY IS THE MUSIC SPEEDING UP?

With my aversion to video games, I fell further and further behind in the gaming world as technology advanced. It's one thing to try to learn swift hand-eye coordination skills on a 1982 PAC-MAN game with an Atari joystick. It's quite another to attempt *Call of Duty* using these new crazy controller contraptions with all the touch-sensitive buttons and headsets.

If I played *The Oregon Trail* today, I would be the first one to die of dysentery.

If I played *Halo* or *World of Warcraft*, I'd still be the first one to die of dysentery.

The last time I even *attempted* to game, it was some *The Lord of the Rings* adventure years ago. I was attacked immediately. It wasn't even an orc that destroyed me. I think it was a hobbit. Then I died of dysentery.

The reality is that I'm light-years behind in my gaming skills because I had no one to teach me what to do, and even if I had, I had no way to practice.

It's tough to learn a skill when you've never had a guide. But sad gaming abilities are simple compared to the quandary of dealing with generations of spiritual junk.

. . .

King Solomon, David's son, ruled over Israel for 40 years. For most of his life, he was a wise yet tough king. He followed the Lord, as his father had. During Solomon's reign, Israel saw great prosperity and the building of the temple. But, unfortunately, Solomon had a penchant for dangerous women. During his reign, he amassed 700 wives and

300 concubines. Many of these women were brought over from foreign countries and worshipped gods other than the living God. They brought all this spiritual pollution with them into Solomon's household, and it began poisoning his heart. As is usually the case when you allow a gateway to sin, Solomon moved on to a worse thing: He started sacrificing to the fake gods as well.

God was furious with Solomon for turning away from Him. He warned Solomon to knock it off, but the king ignored His command. Finally, God had seen enough. He told Solomon, "Since you have not kept my covenant and have disobeyed my decrees, I will surely tear the kingdom away from you and give it to one of your servants" (1 Kings 11:11). Yet God had loved Solomon's father, David, so much that He decided to wait to throttle the kingdom until after Solomon's death.

After Solomon died, his son Rehoboam took his place as king, but apparently the wisdom God had given to Solomon wasn't passed down to him. Once he took over, he gathered the people, and the people said, "Hey, listen, about your dad. He was a harsh taskmaster and worked us too hard. If you agree to take it easy on us, we will gladly serve you." Rehoboam consulted his father's advisers, and they counseled him to acquiesce to the people.

But Rehoboam didn't listen. Instead, he turned to the buddies he grew up with. They all advised him to come down hard on his kingdom. He followed their advice and told the people, "If you think my father was tough, you haven't seen anything yet. My father used whips, and I'm going to discipline with scorpions!" (For Pete's sake, Rehoboam, read the room a little.)

This tirade did not go over well with the people. (Shocker.) The kingdom divided into two after a revolt. Rehoboam—and with him, the dynasty of David—took control of Judah. The kingdom of Israel was now ruled by a man named Jeroboam.

Although the two kingdoms went their separate ways, one commonality was passed down from King Solomon's reign: a nasty idol worship problem. King after king after king chose to worship idols and allow evil practices instead of following the Lord. To be honest, while reading through the books of 1 and 2 Kings, you can start feeling trapped on a merry-go-round of evil. It's the same old, same old: Evil king dies, new king takes over, and he, too, "does evil in the sight of the Lord."

Granted, some kings were way worse than others. Some of them actively practiced witchcraft, held séances, and killed their own children in sacrificial offerings. During this time, the temple of God in Jerusalem—the place where true worship should have been happening—fell into terrible disrepair. One king even placed a shrine to a sex goddess in there. A few of the kings still allowed other kinds of pagan worship, like ritual prostitution, but they cleaned up the kingdoms just a bit and got rid of Baal worship. That might seem a *little* better, but at their core, they weren't putting God first in their lives, and they were leading their entire kingdoms to do the same. God was not pleased, to put it mildly.

A large part of the problem was the lack of godly teaching from the previous generation. Kings weren't passing down the Word of God to their children. Instead, they were actively teaching them to sin. A whole generational mess all started with Solomon's selfish disobedience.

Finally, in the kingdom of Judah, a boy named Josiah inherited the nation and became king when he was eight years old. When he was 18, he decided to repair the temple of God. It must have been in bad shape because important sacred artifacts had been lost in its depths for many years. A high priest was rummaging through the temple during the early restoration period when he found the Book of God's Law. He immediately had it sent over to King Josiah.

When King Josiah began reading the book, he was overwhelmed with heartache and tore off his clothes in anguish. He'd had no idea his nation was so off track and had been sinning so spectacularly. He sprang into action.

King Josiah sought godly wisdom on what he needed to do to repent and turn his people around. Then he called the entire kingdom together to hear the reading of the Book of God's Law. He solemnly committed to do whatever was necessary to follow the law of God. The people all agreed and committed to change their ways as well.

King Josiah did not start his housecleaning gently. He had the temple completely purged of idols and then had them burned in a field, making sure to dispose of all the ashes. He eliminated pagan priests and swept the kingdom clean of any form of weird cosmic worship. He smashed pagan shrines and altars and tore out religious prostitution rooms. He demolished a disgusting furnace set up for child sacrifice. Josiah got rid of witchcraft, sorcery, carved idols—all of it. He didn't leave a single remnant of false religion in the entire kingdom.

Then Josiah commanded the entire nation to celebrate Passover together, which had not been done since the days of the judges. Josiah was the king who started this tradition, to remind the people of God's infinite mercy. The Bible says of Josiah, "Never before had there been a king like Josiah, who turned to the LORD with all his heart and soul and strength, obeying all the laws of Moses. And there has never been a king like him since" (2 Kings 23:25).

The story of King Josiah shows us that it's never too late to follow God. True, being taught God's truth by your parents and growing up with good role models can start you on the right path. That's the way life is designed to be. But sometimes, because of one person's selfishness and sin, the whole system can get out of whack.

It doesn't have to end that way. You always have a choice. You can say, "It starts now. It starts with me." You can decide to start following the Lord. You can choose to teach His truths to your children.

At a certain point, you must stop blaming the people who came before you and take responsibility for your own actions. Though it was easy to blame my folks for my pathetic gaming skills, the truth is, if I really wanted to learn to play video games, I could start right now. I could buy one of those machines and maybe have a gamer friend show me how to tackle the controller. I could probably get pretty good at it. It's never too late.

More important, it's never too late for us to make a choice to turn our lives over to God. Every moment is a new beginning, if we choose it to be.

14

PERSECUTION
THE TWILIGHT ZONE

Don't be surprised, dear brothers and
sisters, if the world hates you.
1 JOHN 3:13

was 12 when I flew in an airplane for the first time.

As my family was finding our coach seats, a flight attendant asked my parents if we would mind being bumped to first class. She explained that they needed to "balance the plane," and since our family had the necessary number of members to correct the problem, we had been selected. (Looking back now, this airplane-balancing thing strikes me as concerning. Can planes really teeter-totter? What if there's a toilet rat in the front bathroom of the plane and everyone runs to the back? Could the plane just tip out of the sky? Wait-wait-wait—don't tell me. I don't want to know.)

The other incredible part of my first flight was that an aeronautical engineer sat next to us. Throughout the trip, he explained exactly what was happening with the mechanical noises and vibrations. (I probably should have asked about the airplane tipping issue, but that only just now occurred to me.)

I mean, the only thing missing from that amazing initial flight was free seat puppies.

Yet my first flight was a mixed blessing: Because I first experienced such high standards, every flight after that was a letdown.

I've been crammed next to an arguing couple for the duration of a five-hour flight.

I've been lost in the bowels of international travel. (Once, while trying to work my way through the system, I was stuck in the large intestine section for 12 hours.[1])

I've eaten some pretty disgusting airplane food. (If you think airplane food is bad, or vegan food is bad, or British food is bad, you should try vegan British airplane food. Yes, do. Just go ahead and try it. I dare you.)

I've sat next to screaming babies and judged the parents.

I've held my own screaming babies and judged myself.

All in all, I guess I should just be thankful I've never taken an airplane trip in the Twilight Zone.

In the *Twilight Zone* episode "Nightmare at 20,000 Feet" (Season 5, Episode 23), Bob Wilson and his wife are taking a nighttime cross-country flight. It's Bob's first airplane trip in six months—ever since he was admitted to a sanitarium for having a nervous breakdown on a prior flight. Understandably, his wife is nervous about his mental state as they settle into their seats. Bob assures her he's fine, though he does seem a bit apprehensive.

A while after the plane takes off, Bob's wife falls asleep and Bob grows bored. He glances out the window and is shaken to see a hairy creature creeping along the wing of the plane. Bob quickly shuts the window's curtain and questions his own eyes (and sanity). But the temptation to look again is too great, and he opens the curtain. This time the gremlin is inches away from Bob, staring at him through the glass pane. Terrified, Bob pushes the call button to notify the stewardess, but by the time she arrives, the gremlin has disappeared.

Bob's wife awakens, and her husband's behavior concerns her. Bob knows his sanity is being questioned and that he might end up in the sanitarium again if he continues to warn his wife and the rest of the crew.

---

1. That would be the airport in Frankfurt, Germany.

When no one else is watching, Bob spies the gremlin again, and this time it's tampering with the electrical wiring on the plane's wing. He realizes the gremlin is going to cause the plane to crash. He keeps trying to warn everyone, including the flight engineer, but the creature disappears every time they look. The crew and his wife think Bob is nuts. They attempt to reason with him—and even sedate him.

Bob knows the truth, but nobody believes him.

Finally, he decides he must take matters into his own hands to save his fellow passengers. He stealthily takes a gun from a sleeping police officer and makes his way back to his seat. As the gremlin rips apart the wing, Bob throws open the emergency window and is sucked halfway out of the plane. The creature notices Bob and lunges for him, but Bob shoots him multiple times. As the horrified passengers attempt to pull Bob back into the cabin, the creature finally disappears for good.

Later, after the plane lands, the authorities straitjacket Bob and carry him away on a gurney. Surprisingly, Bob is at peace. He knows the truth—he saved the plane from crashing. The *Twilight Zone* narrator points out that, soon enough, everyone will know the truth because the gremlin's claws have left the wing in shambles. Bob will be proven right after all.

* * *

It can be incredibly frustrating when nobody will listen when you're telling the truth. It's even more frustrating when they actively punish you for it.

Jeremiah was a prophet around the time King Josiah ruled Judah. Even though Josiah had made major headway in turning God's people back to Him, it wasn't quite enough to undo so many years' worth of evil shenanigans. After Josiah died, his son Jehoahaz took over and, *lo and behold*, he turned the people back to a life of worshipping false gods (2 Kings 23:32; Jeremiah 11:10). Imagine getting your house spotlessly clean, only to wake up and discover that your kid has smeared peanut butter all over the walls. Anyway, it was kinda like that, only with human sacrifice.

God was fed up. He loved His people, but He was ready to let them deal with the consequences of their actions. God needed a human megaphone to declare His message to His people. He chose Jeremiah, the son of a Jewish priest.

Jeremiah wasn't keen on taking the job. For one thing, as he pointed out to God, he was young. But God is not deterred by age, appearance, social status, or finances. He knows who's best for the job, and He provides the necessary skills. God touched Jeremiah's mouth and placed His Word there (Jeremiah 1:6-9).

From that point forward, Jeremiah told the truth. And people didn't like that very much.

First, he prophesied the destruction of Judah because of its disobedience. The kingdom would be weakened by famine and then overtaken by foreign invaders. At that time, many false prophets were preaching the *opposite* of what Jeremiah was saying. Greedy fake priests wanted to keep the idolatry train moving full steam ahead, so they told God's people everything they were doing was A-OK with the Lord. Jeremiah called the priests out as liars and urged the people to turn their hearts back to God.

The people didn't like Jeremiah raining on their immorality parade. At the town of Anathoth, men plotted to kill him. God alerted Jeremiah, however, and then He punished the men (Jeremiah 11:18-23).

Even so, Jeremiah complained to God: "You know, this telling the truth is not all it's cracked up to be. I don't understand why wicked people get to prosper and I'm still sitting here—bruised, battered, and mocked." God told him it was only going to get worse.

Jeremiah kept on preaching the truth to the people: They needed to get right with God and stop their evil deeds. But a priest named Pashur had Jeremiah beaten and put in stocks overnight at the Upper Gate in Jerusalem to shut him up (Jeremiah 20:2). When Jeremiah was freed in the morning, he walked right back up to Pashur and told him Babylon would soon capture Israel.

Jeremiah simply could *not* keep the truth bottled up inside him. The persecution he kept facing was immense, but if he stopped mentioning God's name, the Word became like fire in his heart, and he couldn't hold it in (Jeremiah 20:9). It was like prophecy indigestion.

Finally, the king's officials decided they needed to shut Jeremiah's yap for good, but somehow not be guilty of killing him. They and the priests put Jeremiah in a cistern, where he sank into the mud. They figured if he starved, they technically couldn't be convicted of murder. However, a man rescued Jeremiah out of the pit. Then Jeremiah was thrown in prison until his prophecy came to pass: The Babylonians captured Jerusalem, just as he said would they would (Jeremiah 38–39).

The Babylonians treated Jeremiah better than his own people had. They released him from prison and allowed him to decide where he wanted to live. He went to Mizpah in Benjamin for a while, until the next Israelite king fled to Egypt and took Jeremiah with him. For the rest of his life, Jeremiah urged God's people to turn back to Him, no matter where they were scattered (Jeremiah 40; 43).

If we tell God's truth and stand up for what's right, we *will* face repercussions. That's just the way it is. Paul warns us in 2 Timothy 3:12, "Everyone who wants to live a godly life in Christ Jesus will suffer persecution." People might make nasty comments about us behind our backs or even to our faces. We might lose jobs. Our friends and family might turn against us. In some countries, we might be locked up, beaten, or even killed.

Some people just do *not* like the truth, and probably for good reason: The truth isn't always fun.

When we call out injustice, mistreatment, and sin, people might think we're mean. Or crazy. Or they'll look at us strangely, as though we've just said we saw a gremlin. But we're still called to stand up for what's right. Peter warns us not to be shocked when we face persecution. In 1 Peter 4:12-14, he says,

> Dear friends, don't be surprised at the fiery trials you are going through, as if something strange were happening to you. Instead, be very glad—for these trials make you partners with Christ in his suffering, so that you will have the wonderful joy of seeing his glory when it is revealed to all the world. If you are insulted because you bear the name of Christ, you will be blessed, for the glorious Spirit of God rests upon you.

We are called to keep telling the truth, no matter what. But we're also instructed to behave in a certain manner.

BE WILLING AND GENTLE

If someone asks about your hope as a believer, always be
ready to explain it. But do this in a gentle and respectful
way. Keep your conscience clear. Then if people speak
against you, they will be ashamed when they see
what a good life you live because you belong to Christ.
Remember, it is better to suffer for doing good, if that
is what God wants, than to suffer for doing wrong!

1 PETER 3:15-17

Sometimes our truth-telling as Christians can be off-putting.

A man often stands at a busy intersection near my home. He carries a megaphone and places handmade signs next to him that say, "REPENT," "THE END IS NEAR," and lots of other niceties about burning in hell and whom God particularly hates. Frankly, I don't read the signs too closely. They hurt my eyes. And his spelling is not great. When drivers stop at a red light, he stands inches from their car windows and hollers angry accusations into his megaphone.

He might be willing to share what he believes, but his delivery needs some serious work.

I've often wanted to lower my window and ask, "Does this ever work?" I can't imagine being screamed at would make anyone want to find out more about this fellow named Jesus.

When we're called to reveal truth, we're to do it in *love*. And remember, love is patient and kind, not acting like a raging lunatic.

DON'T THROW A FIT WHEN
YOU'RE HIT WITH RESISTANCE

God blesses you when people mock you and
persecute you and lie about you and say all sorts of
evil things against you because you are my followers.
Be happy about it! Be very glad! For a great reward

awaits you in heaven. And remember, the ancient
prophets were persecuted in the same way.
MATTHEW 5:11-12

Sometimes we Christians are shocked when we face persecution because of our faith. We throw a hissy fit and demand better treatment. But Jesus says we should be happy! When we're mistreated because of our love for God, we're joined with Jesus. He is there with us. He understands what we're going through.

We may never find ourselves in jail or in a straitjacket for standing up for our faith. But you never know; it could happen. We don't need to be worried about that, though. We just need to stand firm and speak the truth, in love, moment to moment.

God will give us the words and strength we need.

15

NONCONFORMITY

BACK TO THE FUTURE

Don't copy the behavior and customs of this world, but let God transform you into a new person by changing the way you think. Then you will learn to know God's will for you, which is good and pleasing and perfect.

ROMANS 12:2

W hen the powers that be were handing out jobs, I'm so glad I wasn't placed in charge of the Department of Time Travel Management.

Ugh, all the *rules*. I'd never be able to keep them straight. I'd get fired immediately. I'd be like Lucy Ricardo in that *I Love Lucy* assembly line episode, except instead of shoving chocolates into my mouth, I'd be shoving time travel grandfather paradoxes[1] into space-time continuums. Even if I could learn all the rules, lo and behold, there'd be a new one:

Don't stomp on a butterfly or all civilization will be destroyed.
Don't interact with your past or future self.

---

1. A grandfather paradox is the hinkiness that happens in the present after you tweak the past. For example, if you go back in time and accidentally kill your own grandfather before your parents have been born, then you have essentially eliminated your *own* existence. Which would make your killing your poor grandfather impossible. Which would make eliminating yourself impossible. It goes on and on and on until your head hurts and you just want to sit in your closet by yourself, eating Cadbury Mini Eggs.

Okay, go ahead and interact with your past or future self, but don't tell them who you are, because both your brains will melt.

If you're in charge of eliminating your younger or future self, don't. Just don't.

You can't change the past.

Well, you can change the past, but it's not a good idea.

Okay, you can change the past, and it is now of upmost importance that you do so.

Come on, time travelers. Consistency! But despite all the paradoxical high jinks, I think everyone regards one big time travel rule as gold, and that rule is thus:

Don't become too entangled in the world around you, or you will MESS STUFF UP.

And, of course, Marty McFly did exactly that.

Marty, Marty, Marty! But I suppose we have got to cut the kid a little slack. In *Back to the Future*, he has a lot on his time-traveling plate, and he's just figuring it out as he goes along. Because of a crazy scientist, angry terrorists, and a time-traveling DeLorean, Marty is accidentally thrust back in time to 1955—and winds up meeting his high school–aged parents. Before he knows what's happening, he breaks the one big time travel rule and promptly MESSES STUFF UP. And how exactly does Marty MESS STUFF UP? He causes his own mother to fall in love with *him* instead of with his father. Which is, you know, problematic. If he doesn't get them together before it's time to return back to the future,[2] there won't even be a Marty to return home.

Marty must walk a delicate line. He's stuck in 1955 Hill Valley for a while, but he does have two jobs to do while he's there:

1. Find a power source for his time machine

2. Help his parents fall in love

Two big jobs, but the latter proves to be the tougher task. Before he disappears from existence, he needs to prod his wimp of a father

---

2 Oh, hey! "Back to the future." I just got that.

to get the guts to pursue his mother. But Marty just doesn't belong in 1955 Hill Valley. The more he meddles and immerses himself in his parents' world, the messier life gets. Finally, he finds himself standing in as his own mother's date to the "Enchantment Under the Sea" dance as his very existence is fading into nothingness.

• • •

By trying to fit himself into a world where he doesn't belong, Marty almost destroys himself. And when we try to copy the world, we do that too. But, man, it's so *easy* to get entangled. You might:

Watch a racy movie with friends…

> …just because it's easier than sitting alone in a different movie theater.

Laugh at a racist joke…

> …just because it's easier than confronting the hatred behind it.

Start down the path to drug addiction…

> …just because it's easier than finding a new crowd.

Ignore bullying…

> …just because it's easier to stay out of the line of fire.

Allow injustice…

> …just because it's easier to stand with the powerful than with the weak.

Yes, you face a tricky balancing act as a Christian. If you compromise your faith, you will MESS STUFF UP. But you can't hide away in a cave, either. Like Marty McFly, you have jobs to do while you're living this life. But your jobs are a little different from his. You're called to:

1. Love the Lord our God with all your heart, mind, and soul.
2. Love your neighbor as yourself.

That's basically it. If you're to do your jobs, you've gotta be in the world. That's where your neighbor is. But you're called to love your neighbors *without* copying their bad behaviors.

How exactly is this balancing act accomplished, anyway?

Daniel is a good example of a man who understands the delicate balance between interaction and entanglement. He knew how to love others and love his God at the same time.

In Daniel's time, the Hebrew people were in a world of hurt. Their nation had nearly fallen apart, and they had been dragged to Babylon (modern-day Iraq, which is pretty far from Israel) and were held in slavery there. The Hebrew people tried their best to keep their customs and heritage despite being surrounded by a society that decidedly did *not* worship the living God.

Daniel was one of the Hebrew slaves who devoutly worshipped the Lord. He was also extraordinarily smart, perceptive, and forthright, and he drew the eye of King Nebuchadnezzar because of his mental prowess and ability to interpret dreams. His words and actions were respectful and wise. He quickly rose to the top of the king's advisers. But his faith and religious habits soon drew the ire of the other, less-successful advisers.

You see, Daniel also had two jobs to do while he was in Babylon: serve his earthly king and help him prosper and serve his heavenly Father and worship Him only. Unfortunately, those two objectives were at odds, and over and over he was forced to choose between them. Daniel's story is so remarkable because he always chose God's way, even when it placed him in the crosshairs of controversy and danger. Thankfully, God had big plans for Daniel to influence the world of Babylon, so He gave him strength, cunning, and faith to walk the balance beam.

Daniel followed a strict, healthy diet full of green leafy vegetables, and he continued to follow it in Babylon. His immediate supervisor was perplexed that Daniel refused to eat the same heavy, meat-filled diet of most Babylonians. But instead of throwing a fit to insist on his way or bending to a different diet, Daniel appealed to the overseer's curiosity. He offered a little experimentation game to the steward to demonstrate the benefits of his diet. Soon, the overseer had to admit the results were astounding.

Additionally, Daniel always told King Nebuchadnezzar the truth, but in a respectful, loving way. When the king was perplexed at a disturbing dream, Daniel was able to interpret the meaning for him. He didn't mince words concerning the true meaning: If the king didn't break away from his life of sin and begin to show mercy to the poor, the Lord would force him to live like an animal for seven seasons. The king chose not to heed the dream's warning, but the fact that Daniel wasn't thrown out of Nebuchadnezzar's court shows the extent of Daniel's respect and truth-telling.

Nebuchadnezzar did end up losing his ever-lovin' mind and living like a feral beast in the wilderness. When God finally brought him back to his senses, the king was humbled, and he praised God's mightiness.

The most dramatic of Daniel's experiences happened under the rule of a new king, Darius. The advisers had finally grown weary of Daniel's status as teacher's pet and began looking for a way to get rid of him. They searched for his closet of skeletons, but they found nothing. They realized Daniel's love for the living God was the ticket to his undoing. Knowing Daniel's habit of praying to God three times daily, they manipulated Darius into making a law forcing people to pray only to him.

Daniel had a choice: Give in to the king's demand and pray to a false god or stay true to the real God. For Daniel, it was a no-brainer. He stuck with his usual schedule of worship. The advisers were quick to arrest him and bring him before King Darius. Darius, who loved Daniel, was brokenhearted to sentence him to death in the lions' den, but his authority was on the line. Before he had Daniel thrown to the lions, Darius begged God to rescue him.

Well, thankfully, Daniel's trial had a happy ending. God sent His angels to keep the lions' mouths clamped shut. When Darius found Daniel alive and well the next morning, he was overjoyed. He praised God himself, declaring that all his kingdom should acknowledge God's might.

Daniel did the best he could with the talents and life he'd been given. He influenced his kings, neighbors, and the world around him while staying true to his beliefs and the God he served. If he had eaten defiled food, prayed to idols, or lied to the king, his witness for God would have been invalid.

Daniel served his kings well during his lifetime: his earthly, temporary kings and his heavenly, eternal King. He told the truth and stood his ground. He was involved with his world, but he didn't get entangled. His actions resulted in two of the most powerful men in the world, Nebuchadnezzar and Darius, acknowledging the mightiness of God.

In *Back to the Future*, Marty McFly eventually completed his mission. He helped his parents fall in love, and he got his time machine and himself back to the future.[3] But things could have gone a whole lot more smoothly if he hadn't allowed himself to become ensnared by the 1955 world around him.

Be a Daniel. Not a Marty.

---

3. Hey, look! There it is again!

16

PLANS

LEGOS

You can make many plans,
but the LORD's purpose will prevail.
PROVERBS 19:21

B ack when I was a kid, I had a small set of Legos that I kept in an old, washed-out margarine tub. I didn't have a mountain of them, and I had only a small selection of colors: red, white, blue, and yellow. I don't even think they made orange ones back then.

This was before Legos came in theme kits, and the only directions were something along these lines:

1. Open box.

2. Stack Legos into shapes.

3. Have fun, kid.

I had some basic rectangular blocks, but I also had a few wheel pieces, a door, and some windows, so I built a lot of house contraptions on wheels. I also had a green plastic Lego tree, so that went on top of the wheeled house, of course. I didn't know what I was making, but it always turned out interesting and unique.

Fast-forward to today, and it's a different story with worlds of Lego sets for multiple fandoms. They make Star Wars Legos, superhero

Legos, and ninja Legos. They even have "girlie" Lego sets now. They come in shades of pink and purple, with kits for pony stables, ice cream parlors, and baby-animal vet clinics. As a woman, I should probably be offended that Lego felt the need to pander to gender-centric stereotypes, but the girl sets come with baby hedgehog Legos! I love me some baby hedgehogs, so there went my righteous womanly ire.

The sets include books with extremely detailed directions. When I was putting together a SpongeBob SquarePants Lego set a few years ago, I found myself mesmerized by the preciseness of the plans. One whole page was devoted to placing a single orange Lego on top of a single green Lego. Making my creation was incredibly easy. I just started on page one, followed the meticulous instructions to the end, and then I had a perfect little Bikini Bottom pineapple house that looked exactly like the one on the front of the box.

It was straightforward.

It was orderly.

It was predictable.

And it didn't have a random green Lego tree growing from the roof.

I'll admit, though, following my no-fail, no-surprise instructions gave me a sense of control.

When we have our plans set out in front of us, we feel safe and secure. We often want life to turn out looking like the image on the front of the box we've created in our minds. We like our own little plans.

God's plans, however, are rarely laid out in front of us like a book of Lego directions. So often His plans require us to throw our perfectly crafted plans out the window and simply trust Him.

That's very difficult for some of us, and that was certainly the case for Jonah.

• • •

The story of Jonah doesn't waste much time getting to the point. Honestly, we don't know that much about him. He was a regular guy in the Bible, just minding his own business. But we don't really need to know that much about him except this: God chose him to carry out a specific plan.

God told Jonah the people of Nineveh were in a load of trouble. They were engaging in unsavory behavior, and God was done with it. He instructed Jonah to go straight to the city and tell its citizens He was going to destroy them.

Now, you'd think if he'd had God telling him precisely what he needed to do, he'd get it in gear and just do it. After all, God is God. Jonah was not. Jonah, however, went the opposite direction from Nineveh. He hopped on a boat and ran away from God's plan because, you know, running away from God has proven successful on *so* many occasions.[1]

As the boat was crossing the sea, God hurled a great storm in its path. The waves crashed. The wind roared. The entire crew was terrified and chucked all their cargo overboard. They prayed to their various fake gods to calm the storm, but it raged on.

Finally, the captain woke Jonah, who'd been napping in the hold of the ship. He demanded that Jonah pray to his God to stop the storm. The crew grew suspicious about Jonah's role in the current disaster. As they pummeled him with questions about his background, they realized he was running away from God. The sailors were terrified.

Meanwhile, the storm was getting worse and worse. When Jonah suggested the crew throw him overboard, they eventually decided to do it. Fearing Jonah's God, they sent up a quick apology to Him before tossing Jonah into the sea. The winds immediately calmed, and the storm stopped. The men were in awe of God and began worshipping Him. Then they sailed on.

God wasn't finished with Jonah, though. His plan to address Nineveh's sins was still off track because of Jonah's refusal to comply. God sent a huge fish to swallow Jonah to keep him safe...and maybe give him a little thinking time.

And that's what Jonah did. He thought. Of course, because he was trapped in the belly of a fish, I don't suppose there was much else to do besides think about the decisions that had brought him there. In fact, that's probably a good rule of thumb: If you're ever stuck inside a fish, question your life choices.

---

1. Spiritual sarcasm.

After three days of deep thoughts and fish guts, Jonah finally came to his senses and realized he'd been out of line. He acknowledged and thanked God for saving him from drowning. Then he promised to go to Nineveh and preach to the people. God commanded the fish to puke up Jonah onto the beach, which it did (gladly, most likely). God spoke to Jonah again: "Go preach to Nineveh." This time, Jonah went straight to Nineveh.

Once there, Jonah told the people, "God has had it with you. If you don't change your evil ways, He will destroy everything in 40 days." Amazingly, the people listened. When word reached the king of Nineveh, he, too, listened, and then he instructed his people to repent. The entire city dressed in scratchy burlap and stopped eating and drinking. They turned from evil and violence and truly changed their lives. God could see He had reached their hearts, and He decided against annihilating them.

But instead of being happy and relieved, Jonah was angry. He'd wanted to see Nineveh pay for their sins. He threw a temper tantrum, yelling at God, "I knew it! Instead of being harsh and punishing, You're being compassionate and merciful, just like You always are! I'm so mad at You! Kill me now!"

God asked, "What reason do you have to be angry?" (I imagine God just rolling His eyes at Jonah.)

Jonah stomped off to the beach to sulk. It's a bit laughable, really. He was mad that his heavenly Father was *too* kind—too loving, too merciful, too forgiving. He sat there in a snit, pouting. God even grew up a little shade tree to cover Jonah and calm him down. In the end, He reminded Jonah that He is God and He can change His mind if He wants to. He has His ways, and that's all there is to it.

Just like Jonah, we all have plans. They can be big, overarching plans, such as getting married, having a family, advancing in a career, or moving into a nice neighborhood. They can also be as small and mundane as planning to order Girl Scout cookies or plant an herb garden next summer.

Self-help gurus encourage us to write out a life mission statement, brainstorm five-year goals, and even plan our days in 15-minute increments in special planners. There's nothing wrong with those actions; planning ahead is a wise habit.

Sometimes, though, your plans and God's plans don't seem to line up. Maybe you lose that job you worked so hard to get. Or you can't get pregnant. Or your trusty neighborhood Girl Scout never shows up at your door. You may look at your five-year goals and realize they've become implausible or even ludicrous.

These setbacks can be incredibly frustrating, especially when it seems as though God has ripped up your carefully constructed and precise plans and left your life looking like a big, confusing margarine tub of mismatched Lego blocks. Sometimes you just want to shake your fist at Him and go sit on the beach to sulk.

You know what? That's okay. God understands. If you want to stomp and pout, you can do that for a little while. I certainly have done so at different points in my life. I've walked into my backyard, kicked a tree, and yelled to God, "I AM SO STINKING MAD AT YOU!"

But you know what? God loved me anyway. My fit didn't change His plans for me, and He kept on loving me all the same. God loves us even when we're behaving like brats.

Tantrums are allowed, but at a certain point you need to get out of your fish belly. God is God. You may not understand Him, but He loves you, and He's got specific plans for you. *Good* plans for you.

As difficult as it can be to come to terms with God's unique plans for your life, it helps if you remember a few truths.

GOD KNOWS THE FUTURE

"I know the plans I have for you," says the Lord. "They are plans for good and not for disaster, to give you a future and a hope."
JEREMIAH 29:11

God knows your past, present, and future. He knows the special part you're meant to play in His eternal story. His plan does not include abandoning you and leaving you hopeless.

GOD'S WAYS ARE HIGHER THAN OURS

Just as the heavens are higher than the earth,
so my ways are higher than your ways and
my thoughts higher than your thoughts.

ISAIAH 55:9

God sees the big picture. He can see far beyond your small scope of the world. He has a grand vision for everything, which might include connecting you to others in surprising ways. His ways are so far above our mental comprehension that we probably wouldn't understand them even if we could see them.

GOD'S PLANS MIGHT NOT ALWAYS MAKE SENSE

We know that God causes everything to work
together for the good of those who love God and
are called according to his purpose for them.

ROMANS 8:28

So often God places us in confounding situations. No matter how you look at it, the circumstances don't seem to make sense or have reasonable solutions. But He knows what He's doing. He has His own timing. You might have to step back and wait for more details to be revealed.

Sometimes, no matter how hard you try to figure out God's plan, you're called to do something hard and brave.

TRUST

Trust in the LORD with all your heart; do not depend
on your own understanding. Seek his will in all you
do, and He will show you which path to take.

PROVERBS 3:5-6

God knows what He's doing. He can lead you into strange territory and begin building odd situations in your life, yet what He's building is creative, glorious, and part of His wonderful, eternal plan.

Even if it involves a weird green plastic tree sticking out at the top.

17

OUR FATHER
STAR WARS

See how very much our Father loves us, for he
calls us his children, and that is what we are!

1 JOHN 3:1

Ah, the ol' Star Wars chapter.

Betcha think I'm gonna compare the Force to the Holy Spirit, eh?

Au contraire, mon frère.[1] This ain't no Force chapter.

For one thing, I'm a rebel like that. For a deux thing, the Force–Holy Spirit comparison has already been done.

No, I'm going to write about daddy issues.

When I was a kid, my father took me to the movie theater to see *Star Wars: Episode VI— Return of the Jedi.*

A quick aside about my poor father here: He was born the youngest child, with two older sisters, no brothers. He married a woman with two sisters, no brothers. Then he proceeded to sire three daughters, no sons. Even our dog, Betsy Lou, was female. My father's world had a sad lack of testosterone, but he did the best with what he had. He sat through terrible ballet recitals, listened to the *Annie* soundtrack on repeat, and even allowed us to decorate his mustache with bows while he tried to read the newspaper.

---

1. That's Canadian for "Nope, bro."

Sometimes, when the man just couldn't take any more tutus, he would grab a daughter and head out for a Daddy/Daughter Day of motorcycle shopping or synchronized growling. That's probably why he ended up hauling his eldest daughter, who had no prior knowledge of anything remotely Star Wars, to sit in a movie theater on a school night.

I was enthralled by the new cinematic world opening before my eyes. I didn't know what an Ewok was, but by golly, I wanted one.

Even more than being enthralled by the movie itself, I was fascinated by my father's explanations and storytelling. In between eating Jujyfruits, he would periodically whisper the *Star Wars* backstory to me: why Han Solo was frozen in carbonite, what a Boba Fett was, and why that one guy had only one hand.

Honestly, we could have been watching a documentary about strawberry jam and it would not have changed my glee. My dad wanted to spend time with me. I felt special.

Have you ever read the book *Hop on Pop* by Dr. Seuss? It's a fun little book, filled with simple rhyming phrases. On one page, Pat is being instructed not to sit upon "that" ("that" being a large cactus. Oh, silly Pat!). On another page, Mr. Brown is leaving town for some reason. I don't know where he goes, but he comes back with Mr. Black. Honestly, the book doesn't have a lot of continuity, but I still have mad love for *Hop on Pop*.

In one scene, two children gleefully jump up and down on their sleeping father's belly. They happily announce that they like to hop. On top of their Pop. And they do. Though their grumpy daddy sternly chastises them for the aforementioned hopping, you'll notice that he doesn't actually do anything about it. It's like he's just kinda accepted that he's Pop, and he's gonna get hop-ons.

Whenever I read that page (out loud, in my biggest, booming-est voice), I'm struck that we all need a good Pop to rely on. Someone to guide us. Someone to teach us. Someone we can hop on when life seems overwhelming. We need a Pop.

Sadly, though, some of us did not have good fathers.

Let's take Luke Skywalker, for example. What a lousy dad Darth Vader was.

First, before Luke was even *born*, his daddy went nutso dark side. In fact, after his mom's death, Luke was hidden on a distant barren planet just to keep him safe from his own father. Then after Luke rescues his sister from their dad's evil clutches, Vader kills off Luke's beloved mentor, Obi-Wan Kenobi. Darth Vader follows up by destroying everything in Luke's wake and freezing his best friend. He even chops off his own son's hand.

Yes, Darth Vader eventually saves Luke's life, and they reconcile before his death, but before that, Vader spent most of his life setting up his kids for a load of therapy. It was one big, dysfunctional family mess.

But not unlike some of our own.

• • •

Man, some awful fathers are out there. All you have to do is watch the nightly news and you'll be presented with a plentitude of bad daddies:

- fathers who steal
- fathers who hurt their babies
- fathers who are emotionally abusive
- fathers who are sexual predators
- fathers who care more about drugs than their families
- fathers who kill their own kids
- fathers who leave and never come back
- fathers who were never even there to begin with

With so many rotten fathers, is it any wonder that so many people struggle with the concept of a loving heavenly Father?

When I was at an age to begin forming a mental image of who God is, it wasn't too hard for me to make the leap from what I knew of earthly fatherhood to what my heavenly Father was like. My own dad certainly had his fatherly flaws, as does every dad, but I never once doubted that he loved me. His character was kind, gentle, and wise. He listened to me. He liked me enough to take me to a sci-fi movie, explain the plot, and fill my tummy with Jujyfruits.

I now know what I had was rare. Many, *many* people compare their Darth Vader–like father to our heavenly Father's character, which could not be further from the truth.

If you didn't have a kind, loving father, I just want to say I'm so sorry. Sometimes life is cruddy and unfair that way, and we have to grieve those big losses in our lives.

Thankfully, we don't have to figure out God's character on our own. We have the Bible to show us the character of our heavenly Father, who created us and loves us to His very core.

Our Father is kind. "The LORD is like a father to his children, tender and compassionate to those who fear him" (Psalm 103:13).

Our Father is patient. "The Lord isn't really being slow about his promise, as some people think. No, he is being patient for your sake. He does not want anyone to be destroyed, but wants everyone to repent" (2 Peter 3:9).

Our Father is loving. "His unfailing love toward those who fear him is as great as the height of the heavens above the earth" (Psalm 103:11).

Our Father is fiercely protective. "The LORD says, 'I will rescue those who love me. I will protect those who trust in my name'" (Psalm 91:14).

Our Father is gentle. "He will feed his flock like a shepherd. He will carry the lambs in his arms, holding them close to his heart. He will gently lead the mother sheep with their young" (Isaiah 40:11).

Another character trait of our heavenly Daddy is that He is a provider. In Philippians 4:19, Paul reassures us that "this same God who takes care of me will supply all your needs from his glorious riches, which have been given to us in Christ Jesus." No matter your losses, God can provide for you.

Consider again Luke Skywalker. His dad made some lousy choices. Darth Vader chose to go wreak havoc all over the galaxy instead of loving and investing time with the people in his life. Luke was left an orphan because of it.

However.

Luke was not left alone. He was not left fatherless. He was provided men (and even a small, green, backward-talking alien) who raised and mentored him. His Uncle Owen. Obi-Wan Kenobi. Yoda.

And you're not alone either.

You may have lost some big dreams. Someone else's sin or neglect might have left a big Jabba the Hutt–size hole in your soul. But if you cry out to God, He can and will fill those holes, sometimes in surprising ways.

Trust Him and see what He does.

18

SIN

LITTLE SHOP OF HORRORS

The wages of sin is death, but the free gift of God is eternal life through Christ Jesus our Lord.

ROMANS 6:23

Not until I was an adult did it occur to me that musicals are kind of ridiculous.

Maybe it took me so long to figure that out because we sang a lot in my house. My sisters and I had a song for everything. The "Eating at McDonald's" song. The "Getting in the Minivan" song. The "My Little Sister Just Puked in the Minivan" song. Once in high school, I even invented a song about the periodic table.[1] Singing out loud was my normal, so why would musicals be any different?

Then, one day, I was watching a musical about phantoms or serial killer barbers or cats. (Maybe it was about phantom serial killer cats? Who even remembers.) Whatever the case, it dawned on me that reality might not work the way it seems to on Broadway. A lot of questionable decision-making is found in musicals:

- Hey, mister. Stop singing about kissing the girl. Just kiss the girl already.

- Do we really need to hear a song about your hair for the third time?

---

1. It was decidedly less catchy than the puking song.

- If you're having such a hard time with your decision to leave Ohio, perhaps you should seek professional help.

- Girl, you are dealing with some serious workplace harassment. You need to talk to Human Resources, not a chorus line.

- Does it concern you that your entire neighborhood is stalking you with a dance routine? That guy just popped out of your trash can.

Despite my rude Broadway awakening, I still have a deep fondness for musicals. My very favorite musical is *Little Shop of Horrors*, possibly the weirdest play ever created.

Little Shop of Horrors tells the dark tale of Seymour, a poor, awkward florist, who is hopelessly in love with his beautiful coworker, Audrey (who, unfortunately, happens to be dating an abusive and mentally unhinged dentist). One day Seymour buys a mysterious plant at a wholesale plant store in Chinatown. He places it in his floral shop window, catching the public's attention. Seymour seems to be the only one who knows how to take care of it, and it grows and grows. The plant becomes something of a celebrity, bringing fame and money to Seymour—though he is evasive about his green thumb proficiency. Seymour names the plant Audrey II after his beloved crush.

Little does everyone know the horror happening behind the scenes:

> Audrey II: Feed me.
> Seymour: Well, okay.
> Audrey II: Blood.
> Seymour: WHAAAAAAAA?
> Audrey II: Now.
> Seymour: Well, okay.

Seymour, convinced that the original Audrey will never love him without the celebrity of the brutal plant, succumbs to secretly feeding humans to the carnivorous plant. (To his credit, he decides to feed the plant only "bad" people, like the horrible dentist. Which, I suppose, carries a certain thieves' honor…but, no. Still very wrong. Don't feed people to plants. Don't be like Seymour.) As the plant grows and grows, Seymour becomes more and more miserable, yet his soul is still chained to his monster.

We, too, can get chained to a life-sucking monster. But our monster is named Sin.

• • •

Just as Seymour didn't like to discuss why his plant was flourishing, we tend to avoid the topic of sin. We might know what we're doing is wrong, but, dang! It feels so good at the time. Sin gives us a little sick burst of adrenaline, a hit of power, a bittersweet shot of invincibility. In the moment, sin can feel nice. Otherwise, we wouldn't find ourselves so drawn to it.

Sin can bring us immediate gratification—sin like…

- a secret sexual encounter
- taking our anger out on an innocent waitress
- cherishing our year-end bonus more than people
- flirting with a married man
- throwing a coworker under the bus to get a promotion
- worshipping our phone rather than God

The list could go on and on and on.

Ultimately, sin kills. James 1:15 says, "When sin is allowed to grow, it gives birth to death." That's true. Sin is such a destructive force because it turns our hearts away from God. God is full of life and light; sin is death and darkness. We can't face both God and sin at the same time.

Sometimes it feels hopeless when you're overcome with sin in your life. Jesus says in John 8:34, "I tell you the truth, everyone who sins is a slave of sin." That's true too. The chains of sin can seem too strong and heavy to break, but Jesus faced the temptation to sin head-on. And He won.

At the beginning of Jesus's ministry, the Holy Spirit led Him into the wilderness to spend 40 days and 40 nights. While there, He fasted from food. When He began dealing with all the normal physical problems of being hungry, alone, and unprotected from the elements, Satan took full advantage of His dicey state. He began tempting and taunting Him.

Satan told Jesus, "Hey, if You really are the Son of God, turn those rocks into bread."

Jesus told him, "No! The Scriptures say, 'People do not live by bread alone, but by every word that comes from the mouth of God'" (Matthew 4:4).

Satan wasn't done yet. He took Jesus to Jerusalem, placed Him on the tip-top of the temple, and said, "Oh yeah? Well, if You're the Son of God, jump! The Bible says angels will come to protect You, so prove it."

Jesus said, "The Scriptures also say, 'You must not test the LORD your God'" (Matthew 4:7).

Then Satan took Jesus to the tallest peak of a mountain and showed Him all of the kingdoms and powers and riches of the world. He told Jesus, "Look at all that! I'll let You have it if You'll just bow down and worship me."

"Get out of here, Satan" Jesus told him. "For the Scriptures say, 'You must worship the LORD your God and serve only him'" (Matthew 4:10).

Finally, Satan gave up and left Jesus alone. Angels came and took care of Jesus. It was a monumental struggle, but Jesus made it through His clash with Satan.

Through His battles against temptation, Jesus taught us some tactics we can use in our own war against sin.

JESUS QUOTED SCRIPTURE AND TRUTH

Jesus knew the best defense against a spiritual attack was God's Word. He didn't rely on His own sharp arguments against Satan. In each instance, He fought back with the truth of Scripture.

We can do this as well when we're tempted to sin. But in order to have truth to tell, we must first take the time to engrave the Word into our minds. We do this by studying our Bibles regularly. Psalm 119:11 says, "I have hidden your word in my heart, that I might not sin against you." Sometimes it helps to memorize key verses concerning our personal stumbling blocks.

JESUS TOLD SATAN TO GET LOST

Jesus didn't let Satan try to mess with His brain for very long. He knew there was no sense in arguing with Satan, "the father of lies" (John 8:44). Satan excels at deception and confusion. Jesus responded with God's Word until He'd had enough of Satan's nonsense. There was no point in contemplating Satan's enticements, so Jesus told him to leave.

We also don't need to mess around with Satan's bait. You can pretend you're "strong" enough to play around with sin without getting entrapped, but you're only asking for trouble. Quit messing around. Tell Satan to get lost and get yourself to a safer spot.

JESUS ALLOWED ANGELS TO MINISTER TO HIS NEEDS

You can face temptation for only so long before you start wearing down. You also need to realize that certain times are breeding grounds for falling into temptation. Hunger and isolation were exhausting Jesus. He knew He was growing weary and He needed help. After He sent Satan on his way, God's angels came to care for Him. He rested and recuperated. We also need to watch our own emotional and physical states and take care of our needs before we end up making a poor choice.

Jesus made several key choices to keep Himself from sinning. Each time, it took a conscious decision to fight back: out in the wilderness, on top of the temple, overlooking the kingdoms of the world. He made a choice. He chose holiness.

You have a choice for your life too. No matter how tightly sin has wrapped its nasty vines around you, you can repent and let Christ's blood wipe your life clean. No sin is too great for Him to forgive. And

He knows what we're facing. Hebrews 2:18 says, "Since he himself has gone through suffering and testing, he is able to help us when we are being tested."

Sin does not have to be our end.

Even *Little Shop of Horrors* has two endings. In the play's original conclusion, Seymour has let his monster get too big to handle. The alien plant gobbles everyone up and takes over the planet. The poor Skid Row residents become part of Audrey II forever, their faces sprouting out as little buds on its long, twisty vines.

The movie version ends on a much happier note. Seymour saves his love, Audrey, from the clutches of Audrey II, and together they destroy the evil plant. Then Seymour and Audrey get married and run off into their happy-ending sunset.

We, too, can choose our ending. We can keep feeding our sin, remaining prisoner to its miserable appetite.

Or we can fight it, turn to God, and break free.

19

FEAR

CHUCK

God has not given us a spirit
of fear and timidity, but of power,
love, and self-discipline.

2 TIMOTHY 1:7

I am the last person to try a New Thing.

It doesn't matter what it is: skinny jeans, the revival of wooden roller coasters, or bearded dragon lizards as pets. I will have *none of that* until the New Thing has taken me by force.

Usually a sister is involved. "For my own good," she will either sign me up for whatever it is or paint whatever it is into my hair or slip whatever it is into my closet.

The only things I embraced wholeheartedly the moment I laid eyes on them were my children and my cargo pants. My reaction was pretty much the same to each:

> Me, cooing to my newborn: "I am in love. You are the most precious thing I have ever laid eyes on. I will cherish you always. You are forever in my heart."

> Me, cooing to my cargo pants: "I am in love. You are the most precious thing I have ever laid eyes on. I will cherish you always. You are forever on the lower half of my body."

On the flip side of that, when I do finally embrace a New Thing, I am fiercely loyal to the end of time. Generally (except for my children, of course,), a sister has to yank the item from my hands (or legs) way past the time when everyone else has moved on.

Several years ago, true to form, I avoided watching a geektastic TV show on network television called *Chuck*—mainly because it was always on the brink of cancellation. I didn't want to fall in love with a new show only to have it yanked away from me. (Turns out, *Chuck* had an almost psychotic fandom, which saved it from annihilation several times. The show persevered for five seasons, often by the skin of its ever lovin' teeth—and the network's fear of rabid nerd violence.)

Finally, I decided I was ready to try *Chuck* on a trial basis. I would give him a fair shot, but I would *not fall in love*. My geek heart had been hurt by premature cancellations before, so I was guarded.

I watched one episode and became an instant, violent, and rabid nerd fan.

Chuck is the story of a sweet nerd who, through various ludicrous happenings, has a computer imprinted onto his brain. He finds his mind loaded with government secrets and is assigned two lethal spies to protect him. Chuck falls head over heels in love with the beautiful girl spy, who also secretly loves him. Oh, and eventually his brain gets a kung fu upgrade.

It's ridiculous. It's nerdy. It's wonderful.

By the episode "Chuck vs. The Tic Tac" in Season 3, Chuck is beyond simply being protected by his spy coworkers. He's trying to become an actual booty-kicking spy like them. The problem is, his normal human emotions keep messing up his ability to use the computer in his brain. His fear is holding him back. Finding himself emotionally paralyzed in a dire situation, he contemplates taking an experimental drug that will eliminate his fear.

Here's an unofficial recap:

"Chuck vs. The Tic Tac" Season 3, Episode 10

The players: Standard Bad Guy and Chuck Bartowski (thankfully without the unfortunate Season 2 sideburns)

SBG: I'm gonna do something bad.

Chuck: No, Standard Bad Guy! However, I'm conflicted and cannot control my fear.

SBG: Here comes the bad thing!

Chuck: I must stop you. I have no choice but to ingest the No Fear Pill.

(Chuck swallows pill.)

SBG: Oh dear.

Chuck: Booty kick!

(Chuck administers kick to the booty.)

Bam! Kick is administered to booty. Foe is vanquished by nerd. Fear is squashed.

• • •

Geeks, of course, are not the only ones who struggle with fear. We all do. Even members of Jesus's own inner circle—His disciples—had major fear issues.

In Matthew 8:23, Jesus and His disciples were in a boat, heading from one side of a big lake to the other. Jesus had been preaching and teaching nonstop, so He was pretty tuckered out. Just as He fell asleep, a storm hit.

Have you ever been in a storm on the water? It ain't no picnic. It's not like being at home under your cozy bedcovers during a spring thunderstorm. It's crazy scary. Every noise seems multiplied by a thousand. The raindrops sound like gunshots. The wind feels like a hurricane. The boat dips into the water with each gust, and water splashes over the side with a vengeance. It's no fun whatsoever. (Well, maybe it's fun for seagulls. I don't know. But seagulls are kind of jerks anyway.)

The disciples were dealing with major storm issues. The wind was howling, the water was churning, and the rain was drenching them. They were freaking out.

Yet, still, Jesus slept.

Finally, His disciples couldn't take the fear any longer. They wanted the storm to stop, and they knew Jesus could fix it for them. They shook Him awake and begged Him to calm the storm, which He promptly did. Jesus basically said, "Shush it!" to the storm, and it was all over.

Jesus realized, though, that the disciples' true problem—their fear— still needed to be addressed.

"Why are you scared?" Jesus said. "Chill out. Have a little faith in Me."[1]

And He was right. The disciples were never in any real danger. They were on a boat with the Son of God, the safest place to be. If they had paused and had faith in Jesus's presence, they might have calmed down a bit. And, who knows? Maybe they would have enjoyed the ride. Taken a nap. Their real enemy during that dark, chaotic boat ride was not the storm; it was their fear.

Fear can nail any of us. It creeps up on us whether we're faced with jaw-dropping obstacles or simply having a rough day. It slips in when we're tired, worn down, and unsure of our next steps. When we face confusion and loss, fear is there, lurking.

Fear whispers in our ear that our God is absent, that we're all alone in this thing called life. It tells us we're going to lose everything dear to us, and that we have no protector, no advocate, and no hope. It hisses that we'll be overtaken, so we should just give up now.

NOPE.

Fear can go take a long hike off a short turnip cart.[2]

God did not give us a spirit of fear and timidity. That junk is not from Him.

Stop and examine whatever is hissing through your mind. God's Spirit is loving, assuring, bold, and powerful. Is that the message? If not, then it's not from Him.

We're always going to have storms in life—every single day. We'll have to battle the Standard Bad Guy—every single day. We'll be forced to give evil a booty-kicking—every single day.

---

1. Maybe I paraphrased a bit here.

2. Turnip carts are known for being exceptionally short.

Despite all our storms, however, we have a no-fear pill: God. We must make the choice, every day, to take Him into our hearts and minds. One way to set our hearts on Him is to plant His promises firmly in our minds. If you aren't good at memorizing, try writing down specific verses and keeping them close at hand. That way, when fear starts whispering, you'll already have the truth. God can and will…

Walk with us through tough times. "Though I am surrounded by troubles, you will protect me from the anger of my enemies. You reach out your hand, and the power of your right hand saves me" (Psalm 138:7).

Provide for our needs. "Don't worry about these things, saying, 'What will we eat? What will we drink? What will we wear?' These things dominate the thoughts of unbelievers, but your heavenly Father already knows all your needs. Seek the Kingdom of God above all else, and live righteously, and he will give you everything you need" (Matthew 6:31-33).

Forgive us. "If we confess our sins to him, he is faithful and just to forgive us our sins and to cleanse us from all wickedness" (1 John 1:9).

Give us wisdom when we need it. "If you need wisdom, ask our generous God, and he will give it to you. He will not rebuke you for asking" (James 1:5).

Bring an eventual end to pain and suffering. "He will wipe every tear from their eyes, and there will be no more death or sorrow or crying or pain. All these things are gone forever" (Revelation 21:4).

Grant us eternal life. "This is how God loved the world: He gave his one and only Son, so that everyone who believes in him will not perish but have eternal life" (John 3:16).

These are God's *promises*. He said He's going to do it, so He's going to do it. Period. Have no fear. Our God is good.

20

TREASURE
THE LORD OF THE RINGS

What do you benefit if you gain the
whole world but lose your own soul? Is
anything worth more than your soul?

MARK 8:36-37

had a pair of spectacular shoes in college.

They weren't just any spectacular shoes; they were high-heeled, green, and sparkly plastic shoes. The heels contained little glitter snow globes with miniature Statues of Liberty inside of them. I've never seen their likeness before or since.

Alas, I don't have them anymore. True to their epic-ness, they went out in a blaze of glory. One sizzling summer, they melted while I was wearing them. I was walking on hot concrete when whatever was holding them together[1] just sort of disintegrated. All I could do was salute them for their service and throw them into the trash.

It's probably for the best, though. Bad things can happen when you start to fall in love with material stuff.

Just ask Gollum.

---

1. Fairy spittle? Tibetan yak grease? Who knows?

The Lord of the Rings is a book trilogy by J.R.R. Tolkien.[2] I've heard it's amazing. It certainly looks amazing. It also looks really long. I'll be honest: I have not read *The Lord of the Rings*. I keep meaning to— really, I do. But since I haven't even finished the old *Ripley's Believe It or Not* books in my bathroom, reading the LOTR is probably not going to be happening anytime soon. Thankfully, a New Zealand filmmaker named Peter Jackson decided to make a slightly less long movie series based on the LOTR books, so we'll start there.

LOTR has a lot going on, from elves to hobbits to cranky trees, but it all boils down to one thing: the One Ring.

A long time ago in Middle-earth, a dude named Sauron forged a bunch of Rings of Power in Mount Doom, a fiery pit in Mordor. He created the rings as gifts for the heads of the Middle-earth realms: the Elves, the Dwarves, and the Men. To be honest, I don't know why each faction didn't think to ask, "Now, why, exactly, is Sauron handing out Rings of Power? Could this possibly be a trap? Shouldn't we look into this a bit more?" I guess free jewelry tends to cloud judgment.

Well, they should have been suspicious because it turns out Sauron secretly created yet another ring—a ring so powerful that it ruled over all the other rings. (Sly little booger, that Sauron.) The Men and Elves each decide to fight him, and the Dúnedan king of Gondor, Isildur, chops off Sauron's ring finger and makes off with the One Ring. He intends to destroy the ring, but he becomes corrupted by its power and keeps it. The ring, though, decides it doesn't like Isildur and hightails it away from him, leaving him vulnerable to orc poison arrows. No more Isildur.

The One Ring remains hidden for 2,500 years, until it's found by two simple Stoor Hobbits, Déagol and Sméagol. The power of the ring overtakes Sméagol, and he kills Déagol to possess it. Sméagol obsesses over the ring for 500 years, stroking it and calling it his "preciousssssss." The malevolent ring slowly turns him into a vile, decrepit creature

---

2. Okay. I've been informed by a Tolkienite that it's not a trilogy. It's really one novel, published for convenience in three volumes. Put down your pitchforks and stop hounding me, you crazed Tolkien fans. Or rather, put down your Anglachels (you know, your angry iron sword forged from a flaming black meteorite by Eol the Dark Elf).

called Gollum. He becomes a shell of the hobbit he once was, utterly devoted to his treasure.

After some time, the ring gets bored with Gollum and leaves him as well, leading to a chain of events, whereupon it is eventually placed in the care of a young hobbit named Frodo. Frodo finds himself charged with returning the One Ring to the fires of Mount Doom, the only place where it can be destroyed. It doesn't take long, however, for the obsessed and distraught Gollum to track down his beloved ring and use every manipulation he can muster to possess his precious again.

Gollum cheats. Gollum lies. Gollum attempts murder. He follows the ring to the ends of Middle-earth, desperate to hold it one more time. In the end, though, Gollum meets the same fate as the ring, consumed by the fires of Mordor. His treasured possession took everything of value in his life, even his very soul.

All because of one dumb ring.

• • •

We are surrounded by stuff.

Stuff fills our homes, cars, and backyards. We have dehydrators and grape-scented candles and state-of-the-art socks and garden gnomes and baby-wipe warmers and life-sized Connect Four games and yogurt makers and kitty condos and Civil War memorabilia and Kermit the Frog dolls and fizzy bath bombs in every color of the rainbow. We've got so much stuff that we must buy or rent bigger stuff to house our excess stuff.

It's not that owning stuff is bad, per se. We need some things to survive. We need food to eat. We need protection from the elements. We need clothes to wear so we aren't running around cold and naked. (Unless cold and naked is your thing. But it's not my thing, so have fun with that.) In any case, stuff is a necessary part of living.

But there's a real difference between having stuff and worshipping stuff.

Jesus warned us of the dangers of materialism in Matthew 6:24: "No one can serve two masters. For you will hate one and love the other;

you will be devoted to one and despise the other. You cannot serve God and be enslaved to money."

Jesus was trying to warn us, because He knew that materialism is like spiritual kudzu.

Kudzu is a creeping plant native to Asia, particularly to Japan. It was brought to the United States many years ago, with the promise to southern farmers that it would help stop soil erosion. However, farmers didn't realize how rapidly the kudzu would take over its new environment. It climbed, crept, and covered millions of acres of land, destroying a lot of American plant life.

From a distance, kudzu looks nice, green, and pretty. It spreads over hillsides like a blanket of leaves. Under its surface, however, it's killing all other plants and trees. Kudzu blocks access to sunlight and other necessary resources, until it eventually takes over farmland entirely. It's lovely, but it's a killer.

Materialism is the same way. First Timothy 6:9-10 says, "People who long to be rich fall into temptation and are trapped by many foolish and harmful desires that plunge them into ruin and destruction. For the love of money is the root of all kinds of evil. And some people, craving money, have wandered from the true faith and pierced themselves with many sorrows."

When you begin letting love of money and material belongings take over your heart and mind, it starts covering your whole life. It steals time and energy from life's essentials. It keeps you from loving and focusing on God. Worshipping objects will kill your soul and turn you into a shell of person.

Yes, materialism will Gollum-ize you.

I started battling against materialism several years ago. At the time, I certainly didn't consider myself "materialistic." I didn't have champagne wishes and caviar dreams, so I figured I didn't have a problem. And even if I *did* have a lot of stuff—hey, didn't everybody? I was no different from any other modern American, was I? But my thinking was just a rationale to try to get myself off the hook. I had allowed a fixation with ownership to invade my mind and my home.

Mine was more of the sentimental materialism problem. If an

object had once meant something to me, I kept it. I saved DVDs of movies that had once resonated with me, nostalgic knickknacks, and old baby clothes. I stashed art supplies that would never be used again. I was particularly fond of my large book collection. I wouldn't admit it, but I was using things to try to define who I was. Piles and piles of them, all so neatly arranged. My home may not have looked like the chaotic house of a hoarder, but my heart sure did.

My conviction started as a gnawing inkling that my life was being wasted on wrangling material items. I spent so much of my time looking after the unimportant that it was to the detriment of the important. I was cleaning stuff. And moving stuff. And rearranging stuff. And buying stuff to organize my stuff. And trying to make more money so I could buy more stuff, which I would *also* clean and move and rearrange.

Then one day I just didn't want to do it anymore. I had been organizing my closet one morning, wiping some dust off a pair of cute Mary Jane high-heeled shoes. It occurred to me that it wasn't the first time I'd wiped a layer of dust off these shoes. Then I realized I had never even *worn* them. Why was I letting these shoes occupy space and mental energy in my life? They added nothing—not one thing.

I began to purge.

I started small. I got rid of the easy items that didn't mean much to me. I got rid of old wool sweaters from high school and dusty cassette tapes. I hauled away boxes of half-finished art projects. At first, some of the items were tough to part with, but much to my surprise, I haven't missed anything I've let go. The decisions may have been difficult at the time, yet living without the stuff has been a huge relief.

Breaking myself free of stuff didn't happen overnight, and I'm still not completely there. For one thing, I live with two small human beings who like stuff very much. They don't yet share my minimalistic convictions. I could probably build a small raft with the amount of foam Nerf darts that cover my house. I'm at a point, however, where I appreciate what I have, and very little is left in my possession that isn't either useful or meaningful.[3]

---

3. Or covered in chocolate. But the chocolate stuff doesn't last long around me.

Now I dream of a way of life that centers on relationships, new adventures, and seeing what God has in store for me. Not dragging along old material burdens.

I think changing our habit of mindlessly collecting stuff hinges on a simple question we must ask ourselves: *What do I treasure?*

- Time for peace and prayer?
- Helping others?
- Building relationships?
- Loving God?
- Or stuff?

Lasting change might mean asking yourself that question repeatedly. I know that's what I have to do. Daily. Every time something new wants to enter my life and home, I find myself asking, *Will this take away from my real treasure?*

Most of the time, the answer is yes, so out it goes. Jesus asks us, "And what do you benefit if you gain the whole world but lose your own soul? Is anything worth more than your soul?" (Mark 8:36-37). I'm sorry, but no mansion, no knickknack, and no glimmering ring is worth the loss of my soul.

Figure out what is truly precioussssssss and put your heart there.

21

ANGER
ANGRY BIRDS

Understand this, my dear brothers and sisters: You must all be quick to listen, slow to speak, and slow to get angry. Human anger does not produce the righteousness God desires.

JAMES 1:19-20

I'm usually a fairly chill person.

I don't get wound up when plans change.

Sometimes we eat popcorn for dinner, and that's cool.

A broken object is not the end of the world in my house.

But you *don't* mess with my babies. That's where my chillness ends. If you mistreat my kids, you will see my mama-bear fury rain down on you like a grizzly battling a lawn chair.[1]

One summer I was at a McDonald's in Arizona. If you've experienced "summer Arizona," you know it's stinking hot. If you want your three-year-old daughter to run off some steam, you take her to the McDonald's indoor play area and hope she makes some friends. Which is what I was doing.

I watched my social daughter crawl up the tall plastic tubes and attempt to befriend some older girls. Before long, I noticed those girls

---

1. Little-known fact: Grizzly bears do not like lawn chairs.

were not speaking kindly to her. They were *bullying* her. I looked over at their mothers, who looked uninterested. When I heard more bullying, I shot more furious glares at the mothers, willing them to intervene. They obviously noticed the bullying, but just as obviously they had no immediate plans to discipline their offspring.

I heard one last taunt hurled at my daughter, and that was *it*.

I marched over to the play structure and climbed up through those narrow, sticky tubes until I reached the kids at the very top. I gave the older girls a firm scolding they weren't going to forget for a while. (I hope they still haven't forgotten.) They sheepishly made a beeline out of the play area, and their embarrassed mothers quickly followed.

I know I looked ridiculous—I was a grown woman crammed into those play tubes overlooking the entire restaurant. But I didn't care one bit. You don't mess with my babies.

It's probably why I'm such a fan of the game *Angry Birds*. If evil green piggies stole my eggs, I would be furious as well.

Angry Birds is a game by the Finnish company Rovio, originally developed for touch-screen smartphones. It's a simple little game that took the world by storm.

The premise? Evil green piggies have stolen eggs from a bird flock. The piggies mockingly snort while sitting inside of and on top of various structures. The player's job is to launch birds at the enemy piggies to smash them. The piggies can be squashed by hitting them directly or by collapsing the structure that contains them.

The birds themselves have different destruction capabilities. Some birds simply land a direct hit. Other birds boomerang, split into three, or drop exploding egg bombs.[2] My favorite guy puffs out like a blowfish when he hits his mark.

Each level is progressively more complicated. The piggy structures are increasingly complex and made from stronger material. Sometimes it takes multiple attempts to figure out how to destroy a piggy habitat or which trajectory angle is needed. Adding to the frustration, some of

---

2. The egg-bombing bird disturbs me. She is protecting her eggs by smashing *more* eggs? Wait... what? It's like when Woodstock the bird eats turkey during *A Charlie Brown Thanksgiving*. I don't want to think about that too much, thanks.

the evil green piggies are tenacious little boogers. Some wear helmets and require several hits to the noggin before they die. Other piggies are extra fat and hard to smash.

One thing is for certain: To win against the piggies, you must be precise with your aim. You can't launch birds all willy-nilly. If you become frustrated and start firing them haphazardly, you'll never accomplish your goal. Keeping your cool and having a steady hand is key.

We could probably take a lesson from *Angry Birds* in how to handle our own anger.

● ● ●

Anger is often portrayed as a negative emotion. When we think of anger, we often imagine someone flying off into a rage, tearing a room apart, or screaming in someone's face. But those acts are not anger; they're *expressions* of anger. Anger is simply a strong feeling of displeasure.

God gave us emotions—even anger—for a purpose. Anger itself is not the problem. The problem is what we do with it.

Even Jesus became angry. The story of His encounter with anger is presented in three of the four Gospels (Matthew 21:12-13; John 2:13-22; and Mark 11:15-18).

Jesus was visiting the temple in Jerusalem during the time of Passover. When He entered the temple, He found men selling pigeons and sheep and oxen, as well as money changers. People were also carrying their goods through the temple.

Jesus was furious.

He wasn't just angry that money handling was happening in a place that should have remained pure and devoted to God; He was angry that the vendors were exploiting tired and weary people who had traveled from afar to worship God at the temple. Price gouging and swindling were going on, all in God's name. Jesus was irate that people were dragging God into a cesspool of greed.

Jesus told off the vendors, declaring, "Get these things out of here. Stop turning my Father's house into a marketplace!" (John 2:16). He released the animals being sold for offerings and knocked over the vendors' tables. He dumped the money on the floor. He refused to allow anyone to carry goods through the temple.

Jesus was angry, and He meant business. He showed us it's okay to experience the emotion of anger. Sometimes anger is necessary to propel us into implementing changes in our lives, but we do need to deal with our anger in healthy and godly ways.

BE SURE YOUR ANGER HAS A CORRECT MOTIVATION

You who love the LORD, hate evil! He protects
the lives of his godly people and rescues
them from the power of the wicked.
PSALM 97:10

We really *should* be angry about some stuff, such as having our eggs stolen by evil green piggies. Jesus wasn't angry that He'd been personally offended while at the temple. He was angry that God was being disrespected. That was a pretty good reason to get angry.

Plenty of immoral things are happening in this world, and they deserve our anger. Things like:

- human trafficking
- child abuse
- the exploitation of powerless people
- domestic violence and verbal abuse
- the perversion of God's Word through cults

If you *aren't* angry about these sorts of things, that's a real problem.

TAKE ONLY CONTROLLED AND FOCUSED ACTION

Control your temper, for anger labels you a fool.
ECCLESIASTES 7:9

Just as in *Angry Birds*, launching your anger with wild abandon is a terrible idea. If you fly off the handle, you can do more harm than good. You might also ruin any opportunity you might have had to make a difference.

Jesus's confrontation in the temple was specific to the acts of defilement around Him. He wasn't abusive in His reaction. He didn't drag up every little thing that each vendor and money changer had ever done wrong in his lifetime, though He easily could have. He simply did what needed to be done. He eliminated the corrupt buying and selling and made a stand for God.

Confrontation can be a delicate matter. We need to deal with the issue at hand, but not deliver a personal attack. We're initially called to confront as privately and respectfully as possible. If change doesn't happen, then we involve others and go public. Jesus says in Matthew 18:15-18,

> "If another believer sins against you, go privately and point out the offense. If the other person listens and confesses it, you have won that person back. But if you are unsuccessful, take one or two others with you and go back again, so that everything you say may be confirmed by two or three witnesses. If the person still refuses to listen, take your case to the church. Then if he or she won't accept the church's decision, treat that person as a pagan or a corrupt tax collector."

Unfortunately, some people have taken these words to mean we should sweep things under the carpet or keep secrets for a perpetrator. Even Christian organizations have been guilty of doing so. That isn't what Jesus meant. For instance, if you know of an instance of child abuse, you should involve someone else so that wrong can be confronted immediately.

Sometimes the first right step is calling the authorities. A perpetrator's privacy or potential embarrassment doesn't take priority over a victim's protection. Proverbs 31:8-9 says, "Speak up for those who cannot speak for themselves; ensure justice for those being crushed. Yes, speak up for the poor and helpless, and see that they get justice."

BE ANGRY FOR ONLY THE PROPER DURATION

"Don't sin by letting anger control you." Don't
let the sun go down while you are still angry,
for anger gives a foothold to the devil.

EPHESIANS 4:26-27

Angry Birds has a limited response time. You're given a certain number of birds to launch, and then you have to take a break and regroup. You can't keep launching birds indefinitely. Likewise, our anger should not go on forever.

After Jesus dealt with the situation in the temple, it was over. He walked away. He didn't allow His anger to turn into bitterness.

Letting anger sink deep into your soul is a good way to ruin your own life. Bitterness can harden your heart very easily, if you let it. As important as it is to feel our anger, it's equally important to know when to let it go and move on.

Feel your anger, act with righteousness, and then let it go.

Sometimes, as much as we try to set things right, we just can't for some reason. We can't make things "fair." The pigs steal our eggs, and then they're gone.

Witnessing unchecked injustice can be maddening. It can be enough to make you seek revenge. But remember that God is in charge, and He knows what's what. In Romans 12:19-21, Paul instructs us, "Dear friends, never take revenge. Leave that to the righteous anger of God. For the Scriptures say, 'I will take revenge; I will pay them back,' says the LORD. Instead, 'If your enemies are hungry, feed them. If they are thirsty, give them something to drink. In doing this, you will heap burning coals of shame on their heads.' Don't let evil conquer you, but conquer evil by doing good."

We're called to act with integrity even if the other person involved does not. We're still called to treat perpetrators with respect, despite their not returning the courtesy.

Just know that, through it all, God understands. He knows what happened. He has not forgotten.

He will *always* keep fighting for us.

22

CHILDREN
STAR TREK:
THE NEXT GENERATION

I tell you the truth, unless you turn from your sins
and become like little children, you will never
get into the Kingdom of Heaven. So anyone
who becomes as humble as this little child
is the greatest in the Kingdom of Heaven.

MATTHEW 18:3-4

"But I've already written one chapter on *Star Trek*," I said, protesting my Trekkie sister's demand.

"It needs two," she said.

"Well, that's not really fair to the other chapters. They might get jealous."

"You will write two chapters about *Star Trek*, or there will be retribution."

And so, because of the threat of nerd revenge, we have arrived at the second *Star Trek*–themed chapter of this book.

Star Trek: The Next Generation follows the crew of the starship USS *Enterprise* as they venture to discover new life and create relationships with alien creatures. Timeline-wise, the adventures are set about 100 years (give or take) after the last mission of the *Enterprise*, led by

Captain James T. Kirk. Jean-Luc Picard is now captain of the starship,[1] with Commander William Riker second-in-command.

In the episode "Rascals" (Season 6, Episode 7), Captain Picard and his crew find themselves in a terrible predicament.[2] While returning to the *Enterprise* after shore leave, Picard and three of his crewmembers encounter turbulence in some sort of energy field.[3] After they're sent back to the *Enterprise* via emergency transport, everyone is shocked to discover the four adults have reverted to their childhood bodies.

Although they appear as children, they still have the mental capabilities of their true adult selves. Yet the rest of the crew can't seem to take seriously the pint-sized versions of their leaders. Picard relinquishes control of the ship to Commander Riker. As the ship's doctor and officers attempt to find a solution, Picard and the other "kids" are forced to come to terms with living life as children. Several of them have trouble reconciling the change: the loss of power, loss of routine, and loss of established roles.

Soon, though, the ship is commandeered by Ferengi pirates, a particularly doofus bunch of aliens. After taking control of the *Enterprise*, the pirates beam most of the adults to a neighboring planet, leaving the children aboard the ship. Before being taken hostage, Commander Riker, who has been allowed to stay onboard, manages to lock the Ferengi out of the computer system.

Sequestered in a school classroom, Picard and his fellow "kids" realize they must behave like true children to save the day. First, they crawl through Jefferies tubes (narrow tunnels through the starship) to get out of the classroom. Then they lure a Ferengi pirate away from the transporter room with the use of a remote-controlled car. Finally, little Picard feins a massive temper tantrum, demanding to see his "father"— Commander Riker. After he's brought to a confused Riker, Picard asks him to turn on some "electronic games" in the classroom. Riker

---

1. Technically, it's a new ship. Actually, if you want to talk for hours with a Trekkie, there are multiple ships if you take into account alternate timelines and mirror universes. Bring a bag of chips for the marathon discussion, though.

2. Terrible predicaments are not uncommon on *Star Trek*.

3. Energy field problems are also not uncommon on *Star Trek*.

understands Picard's plan for rebellion against the pirates and secretly transfers control of the computer system to the classroom.

It works. The children's simple scheme proves effective in trapping the Ferengi invaders into a special force field, allowing the "kids" to regain control of the ship. In finally accepting their child status, the four crew members defeat the aliens and save the day. When the doctor sends them through the modified transporter, they also regain their adult bodies. Everything returns to normal.[4]

• • •

In today's fast-paced world, children are expected to grow up extra quickly. They're spending less and less time making mud pies and playing Red Rover. Long before adulthood, some are worried about starting a diet or building their number of followers on social media. They're inundated with societal messages to act and dress older than they are—to skip the character-building early years and head straight into adulthood.

But Jesus appreciated letting children be children, even though His crew needed some help seeing it that way.

At certain times in the Gospels, Jesus's disciples seemed to forget their place in His inner circle. He wanted them to live with Him and learn from Him, but not be His bodyguards. Yet sometimes they slipped into "entourage" mode.

One time when Jesus was out preaching, He was surrounded by a group of little children. The disciples thought the kids weren't worth Jesus's time, so they scolded them and tried to shoo them away.

Jesus reprimanded His disciples by saying, "Let the children come to me. Don't stop them! For the Kingdom of God belongs to those who are like these children. I tell you the truth, anyone who doesn't receive the Kingdom of God like a child will never enter it" (Mark 10:14-15).

Then Jesus drew the kids to Him, laid His hands on them, and blessed them. It was a small act, but truly a monumental moment.

---

4. Everything returning to normal is not uncommon on *Star Trek*.

Sometimes when we read the story of Jesus with the children, we picture the encounter like an image found in a 1950s Sunday school storybook: A clean, well-groomed Jesus is sitting in a field of tulips with cute children quietly sitting on His lap or at His feet, ignoring the butterflies lightly landing on their toes. They smile angelically and keep their hands folded.

It's a nice image, which makes for a great oil painting, but I suspect it's a bunch of hooey. Because…have you ever met a child?

Real kids are wiggly.

Real kids belch.

Real kids are grubby and covered with dirt and snot and melted Popsicles.

Jesus knew the reality of being a child, and it wasn't like the fake scene in a Sunday school painting. He saw the messy, squirmy, interrupting, giggling, paste-eating wiggle warts up close.

He also said *that's* what we need to become like to enter the kingdom of heaven. That might be one of the more shocking things Jesus said, come to think of it.

Maturity certainly is valuable in our adulthood, but honestly, sometimes our seriousness can get in the way of our spiritual lives. Just like the crew of the starship *Enterprise* did, we must embrace our childlike spirit to thrive.

What does that really mean—to become like a child? Does it mean we need to quit our jobs and sculpt Play-Doh all day? Throw tantrums when we don't get our way? Refuse to brush our teeth unless forced? Er, no. Some behaviors are best left in childhood, where they belong.

Jesus was referring to some of the wonderful core traits of being a child. He wants us to incorporate those marvelous childlike attributes into our spiritual lives. But sometimes we have to ask ourselves what that looks like.

CHILDREN ARE RAMBUNCTIOUS

Children run, climb, and barrel through life with gusto.

They GO, GO, GO full steam ahead until they can't go anymore.

They take a nap, and then GO again.

Are you active in your faith journey? Or stagnant?

CHILDREN ARE INQUISITIVE

Children ask the hard questions.
They explore and are open to new adventures.
They try to figure out new solutions to old problems.

Do you challenge the status quo? Or are you content with the way things are?

CHILDREN ARE RESOURCEFUL

Children take what they have and get creative with it.
They make the most of the day they've been given.
They don't let naysayers get them down.

Are you resourceful in starting new endeavors? Or are you waiting around for the perfect opportunity before you begin to live?

CHILDREN ARE UNABASHED

Children hop up on your lap, press their faces to yours, and yell, "I LOVE YOU!"
They tell it like it is, even if it might get them in trouble.
They keep trying, even when trying seems pointless.

Do you speak unabashedly? Or do you hold back your words in fear?

CHILDREN ARE FULL OF WONDER

Children consider the possibilities.
They are amazed by God's creation—a firefly, the sound of a waterfall, the tide.
They appreciate, imagine, and dream.

Do you wonder? Have you stopped noticing the miracles that surround you?

CHILDREN ARE TRUSTING

Children have sincere confidence in those they love.
They believe when everyone else says believing is silly.
They hold you to your word.

Is doubt holding you back? Are you willing to step out in faith and trust God to do the impossible?

Today, take a break and get back in touch with the childlike spirit God gave you. Ask, "Why?" Sing a song at the top of your lungs. Press your face against God and yell, "I LOVE YOU!"

This could change your life.

23

GIFTS
UHF

God has given each of you a gift from
his great variety of spiritual gifts. Use
them well to serve one another.

1 PETER 4:10

What's the best gift you've ever been given?

I should probably say my best gift was something profound, like a touching letter or a handmade memento from one of my children. But in all honesty, my best gift was a vacuum cleaner. That's not romantic or sentimental, but, hey, you haven't met my vacuum cleaner.

I always hated vacuuming before this powerful, suctioning marvel came into my life. Now I get excited when someone crunches chips into my carpet.

"Ooooooooh! ME! Me me me me me!" I squeal as I scamper off to retrieve my trusty vacuum cleaner.

My favorite part is dumping the contents of the clear canister into the trash can when I'm finished vacuuming. With a mixture of delight and horror, I study all the tidbits that were lurking in my carpet. So much wonderful, disgusting dirt is vanquished by the roar of my fearsome machine.

Dirt, I pity you. I am Ellen, The Thwarter of Crumbs.

My vacuum cleaner, like most truly good gifts, was a gift that got better the more I used it.

George Newman got a life-changing gift in the movie *UHF*. Although, at first, he certainly wasn't sure it was even a *good* gift.

George (played by the king of the geeks himself, "Weird Al" Yankovic) is a nerdy daydreamer who jumps from one dead-end job to another. He hasn't made much of his life. He has a long-suffering girlfriend and a best friend who try to encourage him to do better, but he's just not sure what to do next. One day, though, his Uncle Harvey gives George a gift, in the hopes of getting him on his feet: a manager position at the television station he'd recently won in a poker game.

George takes the job and discovers that the pathetic station, UHF Channel 62, is tanking. It's a programming wasteland for old *Mister Ed* reruns and commercials for local stores like Spatula City (a store that sells only spatulas).[1] And it's nearly bankrupt. He tries and tries to turn the station around with traditional programming, like woodworking shows and news programs, but nothing works. Giving up, he hands the reins of his boring children's show to his weird, mop-obsessed janitor, Stanley Spadowski, and heads to a local bar. With delight, George watches a TV as Stanley's boundless energy and his beloved mop turn the failing show into an instant sensation.

Inspired, George lets his unique imagination run wild. He creates new programming like *Wheel of Fish*, *Bowling for Burgers*, and *Conan the Librarian*, using the people around him as the stars. He takes what he has at hand and runs with it. Before long, UHF Channel 62 is thriving and beloved by the town.

When the owner of a major network station plots to buy George's station and put it out of business, George rallies the town to save it from oblivion. He comes up with the idea of a telethon to turn UHF Channel 62 into a publicly owned station, thereby saving it and giving the community a special channel to call their own.

From the beginning, George had many different options about

---

1. Fun fact: During the 1980s, they filmed *UHF* in Tulsa, Oklahoma, and in it, my friend Kelie can be spotted running through the Spatula City parking lot as an extra. Just look for the girl with the big hair. Well, everyone had big hair; it was the 1980s. But trust me, she's there.

what to do with his gift. He could have refused it when his uncle gave it to him and gone back to his deadbeat, disappointing life. He could have taken over the station but just let it slowly run into the ground. He could have kept trying to push mundane traditional programming that didn't fit with his personality.

Instead, George used what he'd been given and made the most of it. He embraced his weird ideas and took a risk that eventually paid off. He made something big out of something small.

• • •

We, too, are given gifts—gifts from God. We, too, must make choices about how to use them. But our gifts are more substantial and eternal than keeping a television station going.

Jesus illustrates these choices with a parable in Matthew 25:14-30. A rich man is preparing to go on a long journey. In those days, of course, there was no internet banking or calling up your investment broker at a moment's whim, but the man wanted to leave his money in good hands while he was gone. He called in his three servants and entrusted lump sums of his own money to them, each according to his assessment of their ability to handle the responsibility. He gave the first servant a large amount, the second servant a moderate amount, and the third servant a small amount.

After the rich man left, the first servant said, "Well, my master gave me this huge chunk of change. Let's see what I can do with it." He went out, took a risk, invested it—and doubled his master's money. The second servant also decided to invest what had been given to him. He, too, doubled the money. By taking a risk, these two might have lost it all and had nothing to give to their master when he returned, but they tried anyway.

The third servant, however, said, "Nope. Too risky." Instead of investing the money, he hid it in a nice, safe hole in the ground.

When the master returned, all three servants showed him the results of his loans. All three were probably proud of the decisions they'd made, but one servant was in for a rude awakening.

The master was delighted by the decisions of the first two servants. They were commended for their hard work and offered even more responsibility within his estate.

The third servant handed back the exact amount of money he'd been given, saying, "I knew you were a harsh taskmaster and didn't like failure, and I was afraid I'd lose your money. I hid it until you returned. Here you go." The master was furious. He took the money and gave it to the first servant, and then he evicted the fearful, lazy servant into the darkness.

We all have gifts from God:

> God has given each of you a gift from his great variety of spiritual gifts. Use them well to serve one another. Do you have the gift of speaking? Then speak as though God himself were speaking through you. Do you have the gift of helping others? Do it with all the strength and energy that God supplies. Then everything you do will bring glory to God through Jesus Christ. All glory and power to him forever and ever! (1 Peter 4:10-11).

God has big plans for His people, so He gave us tools to serve Him and thrive. Each of us has an important role within God's family. Paul says of fellow believers, "Their responsibility is to equip God's people to do his work and build up the church, the body of Christ" (Ephesians 4:12).

It would be pointless if we were all given the same gifts. Many important jobs would go unfulfilled. What if every single person was given the gift of speaking, but nobody was helping? The world would be loud and confusing and obnoxious. Plus nobody would get anywhere because nobody would be out front directing traffic or unlocking the doors. And there would be no cupcakes. I don't want to live in a land of no cupcakes, so I'm thankful that our gifts are as unique as we are.

God chooses our special gifts. We don't get to decide what they'll be on our own. You might even be given a gift that surprises you. You might have always thought of yourself as a quiet wallflower, only to find that you can lay it down and preach like nobody's business. Or even though you're usually a homebody, you're skilled at building houses in third world countries. Or despite being raised with wealth, you can happily survive and thrive with few material possessions. God's ways are funny like that.

God assigns a multitude of gifts of varying types:

- administration
- apostleship
- artistry
- celibacy
- counseling
- discernment
- encouragement
- evangelism
- faith
- giving
- healing
- hospitality
- interpretation of tongues
- knowledge
- mercy
- missions
- pastoring
- prayer
- prophecy
- service
- teaching
- tongues
- voluntary poverty
- wisdom

Whatever gifts you've been given, remember that God is the giver. Every gift is important and purposeful because He deemed it so. First Corinthians 12:4-6 says, "There are different kinds of spiritual gifts, but the same Spirit is the source of them all. There are different kinds of service, but we serve the same Lord. God works in different ways, but it is the same God who does the work in all of us."

Unfortunately, some of us hide our gifts and don't use them. We're scared of failing, imperfection, or embarrassment.

Looking back at Jesus's story, it's easy to feel sorry for the third servant—at first. After all, he kept the status quo. He didn't rock the boat.

He kept the money safe and sound. Why should he be punished for doing the bare minimum? Was it really so bad that he didn't invest what he'd been given on behalf of his master?

Well, yes, but not because he didn't earn his master more money. The problem was the motivation behind his lack of risk-taking. He didn't take a risk because he feared his master. He was scared because he didn't really know his master's character. The master in this story genuinely wanted his servants to trust him, and to succeed when he asked them to care for his resources. Instead, the third servant viewed him as a tyrant who was burdening him with an unwanted responsibility. If I were the master, I would have been angry with the ungrateful third servant as well.[2]

Some of us might also view God as a strict overseer—a heartless disciplinarian who's out to punish us for any little mistake we make. But that's not who our God is! God's character is one of mercy, compassion, and generosity: "The LORD is good to everyone. He showers compassion on all his creation" (Psalm 145:9). He takes great delight in you, and He also wants you to delight in using your gifts to serve Him.

He wants you to be yourself. Like George Newman, when you use your gifts and embrace your real self—even as goofy and weird as you might be—that's usually when the best stuff happens.

It might take a while to figure out what your gifts are. But make no mistake—God didn't pass you over. He's given you the gifts He wants you to use. Use them!

---

2. I also would have been ticked off that there were no cupcakes waiting for me when I got back home.

24

LEGALISM
THE X-FILES

Don't let anyone capture you with empty
philosophies and high-sounding nonsense that
come from human thinking and from the spiritual
powers of this world, rather than from Christ.

COLOSSIANS 2:8

When I studied in Italy for a year in college, I struggled to learn the language. I'm just not good at language acquisition. I once read that the part of the brain that's good at learning languages is also the part that's good at math. I'm apt to believe that because that section seems to be missing from my brain. Or else God filled it with extrastellar fly-swatting skills. (I am *good* at killing flies.)[1]

When I was in Italy, I was lost most of the time. I learned a few phrases to get by, like "*Mi sono perso. Aiuto.*"[2] or "*Ho bisogno di pizza. Aiuto.*"[3] The one thing that helped was discovering Italian-dubbed reruns of *The X-Files* on TV. I had never watched *The X-Files* before, but I was willing to give it a shot, especially if it would help my poor Italian skills. Somehow, it did. Something about the combo of Italian and alien crime-fighting clicked for me.

---

1. I once killed ten flies with one swat. It was epic and, dare I say, a little heroic. Somebody should probably include that deed in my obituary someday.

2. "I am lost. Help."

3. "I need pizza. Help."

When I came back home to the States, I was excited to return to my newly discovered show. I was irritated, however, to discover that I didn't like the voice of the American actor who portrayed Mulder. I preferred my Italian version of his voice. I remained a fan of the show, but, to this day, David Duchovny's voice sounds wrong to me.

The X-Files tells the story of two FBI agents, Fox Mulder and Dana Scully. Working as a team, Mulder and Scully investigate FBI "X-Files": seemingly unearthly cases in the realm of aliens, shape-shifters, and monsters. Agent Mulder fully believes in extraterrestrial life-forms, while Agent Scully, with her factual medical background, is skeptical. Although the partners frustrate each other, they grow to develop a deep trust and friendship.[4]

One of my favorite episodes (and some episodes are a bit dark and gory, so please use discretion) is Episode 15 from Season 6. In "Arcadia," Mulder and Scully move into a posh suburban neighborhood, the Falls of Arcadia, posing as an affluent young married couple. Adopting the names Rob and Laura Petrie,[5] they've been sent by the FBI to investigate a series of disappearances in the neighborhood.

The neighborhood seems too good to be true. Every lawn is perfectly manicured. The homes are flawlessly maintained. The neighbors reach out to the Petries almost immediately and are unusually helpful. They quickly assist their new residents as they move into their home, mentioning that all move-ins must be completed by 6 p.m. Strangely, the rules of the Falls of Arcadia are *repeatedly* mentioned to the agents.

As soon as the neighbors leave for the day, Scully and Mulder begin scouring the interior of the house for clues. The missing former residents have left the home in nearly perfect condition, but the agents still manage to locate a globby substance on a ceiling fan. It appears to be blood, so Scully sends it off to the FBI lab for processing.

Meanwhile, "Rob and Laura" are the topic of discussion all over the neighborhood; everyone is concerned about whether they'll obey all the bylaws. At a meeting at the home of the property owners association

---

4. And, eventually, maybe more. But romance was never the focal point.

5. Oh, *Rob!*

leader, Mr. Gogolak, a nervous but kindhearted veterinarian named Big Mike begs the leader to let him warn their new neighbors about what could happen if they *don't* keep up appearances. Later that night, Big Mike discovers the lamplight on his street has gone out, and he panics. When he goes out to investigate, he's attacked by a black, grime-covered monster and disappears.

Mulder and Scully notice Big Mike's disappearance and mention it to the other neighbors, but they're tight-lipped. Something just isn't right in Arcadia. Mulder decides to push the "rules" to see what will happen. He puts a pink plastic flamingo in his yard. He knocks his mailbox askew. Each time, the offending object is fixed or removed. Finally, he finds a note in his mailbox, warning him to be just like the others...before it gets dark.

That night, Mulder drags a huge, ugly basketball hoop into his driveway. Horrified, one of the neighborhood couples rush over and implore him to drag it back into the garage. As they're arguing, Mulder catches a glimpse of the filthy, terrorizing monster before it disappears into the night.

Meanwhile, Scully reveals the lab's findings: The substance on the ceiling was not blood, but a mixture of ketchup and motor oil. It's basically garbage, and rightfully so, as Scully discovers that the neighborhood is built on top of an old landfill.

Still suspecting foul play, Mulder decides to go digging for the former residents in the front yard, telling the shocked neighbors that he's adding a reflecting pool. Instead, he finds a tacky, decorative windmill, bearing the name of Mr. Gogolak's company.

Realizing that the neighborhood leader is commanding the monster to control residents who don't perfectly comply with the rules, Mulder takes off to arrest him. Scully calls for a forensic team, but the monster closes in on her inside the house. She's rescued by a grime-covered Big Mike (who's been hiding in the sewers), and the monster makes its way back out into the neighborhood. At last, the monster attacks its own master, Mr. Gogolak, and then it disintegrates into dirt. X-File case closed.

Scully and Mulder lived an extreme example, but many of us also live with the suffocating effects of legalism every day. And it's not pretty.

• • •

What *is* legalism exactly? Religious legalism can be so sly that sometimes it's hard to pin down. It can look like a well-dressed churchgoer giving a disapproving look to a jeans-clad teenager who has dared to venture through the church doors on a Sunday morning. It can look like a family member who chastises an abused wife for not being submissive enough. It can look like a preacher who condemns other church denominations from the pulpit. It can look like lots of things.

At its core, though, legalism is when you put love of law over love of God.

I always found it interesting that Jesus had much harsher words for the pious-acting Pharisees of His day than He had for prostitutes. Jesus was *not* a fan of legalism; He abhorred it. In the twenty-third chapter of Matthew, Jesus really goes off on the Pharisees and their brand of legalism. He calls them "hypocrites" and "blind guides" and sticks their noses to the wall:[6]

"You ignore the more important aspects of the law—justice, mercy and faith" (verse 23).

"You are so careful to clean the outside of the cup and the dish, but inside you are filthy—full of greed and self-indulgence!" (verse 25).

"You are like white-washed tombs—beautiful on the outside but filled on the inside with dead people's bones and all sorts of impurity. Outwardly you look like righteous people, but inwardly your hearts are filled with hypocrisy and lawlessness" (verses 27-28).

Legalism, like Mulder and Scully's neighborhood, looks good from the outside, but under the surface, it's just stinky, festering garbage.

In a letter to the Philippians, Paul warns his Christian brothers and sisters to watch out for legalists because they bring destruction. He points out that he knows what he's talking about because he used to be a legalist himself. Paul had been the king of legalism before his conversion. If you were judging him according the law's religious standards, he had every reason to boast. In Philippians 3:4-6, Paul says:

---

6. Rhetorical noses.

I could have confidence in my own effort if anyone could. Indeed, if others have reason for confidence in their own efforts, I have even more! I was circumcised when I was eight days old. I am a pureblooded citizen of Israel and a member of the tribe of Benjamin—a real Hebrew if there ever was one! I was a member of the Pharisees, who demand the strictest obedience to the Jewish law. I was so zealous that I harshly persecuted the church. And as for righteousness, I obeyed the law without fault.

He was telling the truth. If you checked Paul's dossier from back when he was Saul, you'd find a "perfect" example of religious living:

Member of the Pharisee community? Check.

Followed all the rules? Check.

Enforcer of everyone's behavior and appearance? Check.

Punished people who stepped out of line? Checkity-check-check.

Yes, Saul looked good from the outside. Nearly perfect. But on the inside he was a total mess. He loved the law more than he loved God, and that resulted in his persecuting Christians to their deaths.

It would be nice to say religious legalism died with the Pharisees of Jesus's day, but as I indicated before, legalism is still around us today, even in Christianity. You sense it around you anytime you feel an air of burden: anytime it's implied that you're a "good Christian" only when you follow the rules; anytime appearances are more important than mercy; anytime you feel a spiritual weight being heaved onto your shoulders. Jesus Himself said, "The teachers of religious law and the Pharisees…crush people with unbearable religious demands and never lift a finger to ease the burden. Everything they do is for show" (Matthew 23:1-5).

Legalism leads to death—death of our faith, death of our joy, death of our peace. It comes in like a trash monster and devours our spirits.

But we don't have to live that way.

In Paul's letter to the Philippians, he goes further, explaining that all that stuff once so important to him when he was Saul—the accolades, the rule-following, the self-righteous title—mean zilch to him now:

> I once thought these things were valuable, but now I consider them worthless because of what Christ has done. Yes, everything else is worthless when compared with the infinite value of knowing Christ Jesus my Lord. For his sake I have discarded everything else, counting it all as garbage, so that I could gain Christ and become one with him (Philippians 3:7-9).

As soon as Christ entered his heart, Paul realized all the righteousness he'd attempted to store up for himself meant nothing. All that religious rubbish got in the way of the most important thing: knowing Christ's love.

Acting out the "perfect" religious role versus having a real relationship with Jesus is incomparable. It's like comparing bacon to…oh, I don't know, I'm drawing a blank here. See? Nothing compares to bacon. Or Jesus.

Let me ask you some questions:

Are you feeling burdened by religious "rules"?

Do you feel a heaviness in your heart?

Do you feel spiritually suffocated by human expectations?

Well, that garbage isn't from God. You're living with legalism. You need freedom. You need the real Jesus.

Second Corinthians 3:17 says, "The Lord is the Spirit, and wherever the Spirit of the Lord is, there is freedom." If you're struggling to get away from the binds of legalism, ask God to cut those cords. Ask to see His true, loving, forgiving nature. Ask to build an authentic relationship with Him. He will gladly answer you.

Let go of all the rules. Just let God love you.

25

FAMILY
GUARDIANS OF THE GALAXY

Now you Gentiles are no longer strangers and foreigners. You are citizens along with all of God's holy people. You are members of God's family. Together, we are his house, built on the foundation of the apostles and the prophets. And the cornerstone is Christ Jesus himself.

EPHESIANS 2:19-20

B eing part of a family isn't always easy. You have to live with people who snore, steal the last corn dog, and secretly use up your pricey hair conditioner.[1] You love them, but they can drive you batty.

I suppose, though, it beats having no family at all, which was the case for Peter Quill[2] in the Marvel movie *Guardians of the Galaxy*.

Quill is a loner. It's not too surprising, really. Life hasn't been easy for him. He was abducted from earth as a kid soon after his mom's tragic death. Taken in by rowdy space pirates called Ravagers, Quill was raised under the questionable guidance of the Ravager captain, Yondu. Early on, Quill learns to look out only for himself.

---

1. I'm talking to *you*. You know who you are.

2. He also goes by the name "Star-Lord." Which is a completely *fabulous* name. It's almost as good as "Tangerine Woman." Hellooooo, Marvel—I'm still awaiting your call.

Quill's solitary life is about to drastically change after stealing a mysterious orb from an abandoned planet.

Quill is supposed to return the orb to the Ravagers, but he decides to sell it instead. Yondu is infuriated by Quill's desertion and issues a bounty for him. In addition, an evil warlord named Ronan the Accuser wants the orb and sends the green-skinned assassin, Gamora, to retrieve it. Quill is now officially on his own—and a wanted man.

He reaches the planet of Xandar, home of the galaxy-policing Nova Corps, in hopes of selling the orb. Before long, Peter's enemies encircle him. Gamora ambushes Peter and tries to steal the orb, but he proves to be harder to defeat than she thought. A shady bounty hunter named Rocket (a genetically engineered raccoon) and his treelike bodyguard, Groot, also notice Quill's presence. Gamora and Quill battle in the crowded streets for the orb, while Rocket and Groot make a play to kidnap Quill for the reward. After beating the snot out of one another, they're all arrested by the Nova Corps authorities.

Prison is a harsh environment for the four criminals. Quill is irritated by Groot's singular phrase: "I am Groot." Rocket tries his best to appear menacing to the other inmates. Gamora's reputation precedes her, and she's hated by the other prisoners—especially Drax the Destroyer, a mighty warrior who zeroes in on Gamora's ties to Ronan. The other inmates threaten Gamora, but Quill intervenes.

Gamora reveals that she's double-crossing Ronan. If Quill and Rocket can get them out of prison, she has a buyer for the orb, and she assures them she's willing to split the money. The criminals decide sticking together is their best bet—for now. Quill, Rocket, Groot, Gamora, and Drax make a dramatic jailbreak.

Back on Peter's spaceship, the crew is alone together for the first time. They bicker and butt heads as a band of misfits who don't have anything in common but their own self-protection.

Quill's ship lands at a lawless outpost, Knowhere, to sell the orb to a dealer called the Collector. The Collector reveals that the orb contains an object of great power—an Infinity Stone. Witnessing just a fraction of the stone's power, the group is horrified by the potential damage that could result from its improper use. They realize they can't let the stone fall into Ronan's hands or he will destroy the entire galaxy. Even though none of the members have ever acted with any selflessness or integrity, they decide they must do the right thing; deliver the stone to Nova Corps for safekeeping. But it's going to be tough. For a variety of reasons, several people want the group's members dead. The list of enemies includes Ronan, Yondu, and Gamora's jealous sister, Nebula.

The group tries to form a plan, but Drax's questionable decision-making leaves the team in shambles. Ronan steals the Infinity Stone and heads to Xandar to destroy the planet. The group has a decision to make: Are they going to abandon one another? Or will they join together to save the day? Each member sacrifices their own safety to keep the group together. They're beginning to think like a unit. Despite facing sure death, they decide to fight for the Infinity Stone.

They make their way onto Ronan's spaceship and fight like barracudas. They kill Ronan (apparently), but the ship is heavily damaged—and falling fast. As the ship plunges toward Xandar, Groot wraps his mighty vines around everyone, protecting them in a strong cocoon. Knowing the impact will surely kill Groot, Rocket pleads with him to stop and asks why he's sacrificing himself.

"*We* are Groot," responds the gentle giant.

Quill, Gamora, Drax, and Rocket survive the crash, but, sadly, it appears Groot does not. They have little time to grieve for him, though, as Ronan suddenly emerges and prepares to destroy Xandar.

The gang makes one last attempt to save millions of lives, and Quill grabs the Infinity Stone. The power surges in him, and he can barely keep from exploding. One by one, Gamora, Drax, and Rocket grasp Quill until they absorb the burden of power among the four of them. Then they direct the stone's energy toward Ronan and—*boop!*—he's blasted away.

The team is lauded as heroes, and they're soon reunited with a little Groot sprout. (He survived after all.) As they leave for further adventures in Quill's spaceship, the group has morphed from five individuals into something else entirely.

The Guardians of the Galaxy have become a family.

. . .

Just as being part of a biological or adopted family takes some work, so does being part of a spiritual family. When you become a Christian, you acquire a whole new family. For some of us, going from a life of looking out for number one to functioning in a family unit can be a challenge. It certainly was for me.

In my early twenties, I had been a believer for quite a few years, but I'd never embraced being part of a Christian community. I had a few dear Christian pals here and there, but we lived separate lives. They would stop by for a while, but then skedaddle on their way while I went right back to my solitary spiritual life. Among my many friends, Christian or not, I kept my faith private.

One summer I was hired to work at a Christian camp. I still don't know what on earth that camp director was thinking, hiring a girl like me. He interviewed me by phone, and we talked about C.S. Lewis and faith and whatnot. I don't know if I gave any "right" answers, but at the end of the interview, he thought for a while and then said, "I'm going to hire you. I think you're supposed to be here this summer."

I arrived at the camp in late May and immediately felt like an odd-ball compared to the rest of the staff, although not because of anything anyone said or did. All the counselors, administrators, lifeguards, and horse wranglers were lovely. It was just *me*. I felt like I didn't fit in one bit. All these Christians seemed to know the evangelical lingo and were well versed in *Veggie Tales*, side hugs, and DC Talk. I, on the other hand, had just spent a year sketching naked people at art school and was coming out of a hefty depression. This situation didn't bode well.

For one thing, there was all this weird camp humor. For example, after making an announcement over the loudspeaker, you were required to squawk like a stork who was delivering the message from the air. The first time I heard the squawk, I nearly jumped out of my skin. Everyone else carried on like normal.

Inside jokes aside, I was petrified that I was going to be exposed as a fraud, that I wasn't "Christian" enough to be there. My biggest fear was that someone was going to call on me to pray out loud—or worse, pray over me. I had never done that sort of thing in my life, and I didn't intend to start.

Having an artistic bent, I was hired to be the camp videographer. Although I had never attempted video editing, I walked into that job fully confident that I was going to wow with my cutting-edge cinematography skills. I was going to be the Steven Spielberg of camp video production.

It was shocking how very *bad* I was at it.

Seriously. I had no natural talent for filmmaking. None. My footage was full of blurry shots and extreme close-ups. My editing was choppy and erratic. I couldn't seem to properly sync the footage with the chipper Christian pop music.

And I was slow. Oh, so slow. What would have taken a decent videographer a few hours took me 12. As I tried to piece together the camp video for each Saturday morning's closing ceremony, I felt more and more like a fraud. Friday night after Friday night, I sat in a tiny editing room, full of half-eaten bags of chips and salty tears. Most of those nights, I found myself exhausted and alone, choking back sobs at 4 a.m.

I didn't tell anyone how miserable and lonely I was. It was too embarrassing.

Then one Friday night, as I sat in the editing room with tears running down my cheeks, the door burst open. It was midnight or so. In walked Sarah and Jessica, two lifeguards I was getting to know.

Jessica announced that she was going to pray for me—right then and there. Normally, I would have been terrified of some little sparkling pixie of a human bouncing up and praying over me. But I was just desperate enough to let her. She prayed for strength and courage for me, and it was like a huge weight lifted from my shoulders.

Then Sarah and Jessica said they were in it with me for the long haul. They dragged in their sleeping bags and pillows and curled up next to me as I worked. They cracked jokes and cheered me on until I finished that darn camp video. Then we collapsed on the gymnasium floor in our sleeping bags for a few hours until dawn.

For some reason, something changed in me that night—like, *forever* changed in me.

These people—these fellow believers—were my family, and I realized that I needed them like crazy.

I started embracing my Christian family after that. It took me a while, but I stopped hiding and feeling like a fraud. I finally began to relax and enjoy my community. I bonded, I laughed, and I grew. I discovered that God had an Ellen-size hole in His family, and only I could fill it.

The truth is we're all a bit of a mess. None of us should fit in, because we're naturally full of imperfections and willfulness. But because of Jesus Christ's love and salvation, we *do* belong. John says in 1 John 1:7, "If we are living in the light, as God is in the light, then we have fellowship with each other, and the blood of Jesus, his Son, cleanses us from all sin."

God doesn't want us to be isolated. Sometimes you might have a season of solitude, but on the whole you're meant to be involved with other Christians on a daily basis—to grow, to encourage, to share, to love, to challenge. For our family to be thriving, we're supposed to do some of this stuff together:

PRAY, EAT, AND SPEND TIME TOGETHER

All the believers devoted themselves to the apostles'
teaching, and to fellowship, and to sharing in meals
(including the Lord's Supper), and to prayer.

ACTS 2:42

To be a healthy family, we need to touch base consistently. It's important that we reach out when we're hurting, struggling, or joyful. In addition to worshipping and praying, we need to do the mundane stuff together too: eating, chitchatting, laughing, pulling weeds, complaining about black licorice, what have you.

BE GENEROUS WITH ONE ANOTHER

All the believers met together in one place and shared
everything they had. They sold their property and

possessions and shared the money with those in need.
They worshiped together at the Temple each day, met in
homes for the Lord's Supper, and shared their meals with
great joy and generosity—all the while praising God and
enjoying the goodwill of all the people. And each day the
Lord added to their fellowship those who were being saved.

ACTS 2:44-47

We need to be generous with our time, our resources, and our love. When one of us is in need, it's such a relief to know we have a big family who will step up to help. We can even learn to share our pricey hair conditioner.

GROW TOGETHER

Let us think of ways to motivate one another to acts of
love and good works. And let us not neglect our meeting
together, as some people do, but encourage one another,
especially now that the day of his return is drawing near.

HEBREWS 10:24-25

Spending time with our spiritual family also helps us grow. They push us to be the best we can be. They challenge us to avoid being stagnant in our faith. They encourage us to make the right choices and keep going—even when we're facing failure.

I love our Christian family. Occasionally, just like the gang in *Guardians of the Galaxy*, I don't *like* them very much, but man, I love them.

If you're struggling today, reach out to a brother or sister in Christ. You aren't in this alone.

26

LEADERSHIP
THE MUPPET MOVIE

Among you it will be different. Whoever wants to
be a leader among you must be your servant.

MARK 10:43

Years ago, my family took a trip out to Colorado to go skiing. We'd never driven through the American West before, and coming from the tree-filled South, the prairie landscape was brand-new to us. Somewhere around western Kansas, one of my sisters spotted something we'd never seen before: a tumbleweed. We just *had* to have it. Our vehicle full of females begged my beleaguered father to pull over so we could collect it. My mother loaded the tumbleweed into the minivan, and off we went.

Here's the thing about tumbleweeds: They're essentially prickly, clumpy dust balls. They're literally *weeds* that *tumble*. That ball of dirt just tumbled around the van and poked at everyone until my father noticed that Kansas was filled with tumbleweeds and ours wasn't particularly special. He decided he was on a road trip with a bunch of loonies, and out the tumbleweed went to join the rest of its tumbleweed brethren on the prairie.

It can be maddening to be on a road trip with lovable crazies, as both my father and Kermit the Frog can surely attest.

In *The Muppet Movie*, we meet Kermit, a swamp-living frog with a big dream. He wants to move to Hollywood and create movies to make people happy. After some encouragement from a very lost Hollywood movie agent, Kermit picks up his banjo and sets off to chase his dreams.

Along the way, he picks up a menagerie of friends who share the same vision. He meets Fozzie, a bear comedian at the El Sleezo Cafe, who also wants to make people happy. Kermit invites the bear to join his journey, and Fozzie accepts. Fozzie borrows his uncle's Studebaker for the long drive to California, and off they go.

Moving right along, the duo picks up Gonzo and his chicken girl-friend, Camilla, when Gonzo's plumbing truck flips onto the top of their Studebaker during a road mishap. Miss Piggy joins them after a misunderstanding at a county fair's beauty contest leaves her on her own. Rowlf the Dog joins the gang after meeting them at a piano bar. They also join up with Dr. Teeth and his Electric Mayhem Band—as well as their manager, Scooter—who are renovating an old Presbyterian church alongside the road.

Kermit leads the gang through scads of zany circumstances on their trip to California: a wild balloon chase, near lobotomization by a mad scientist, and an encounter with a sarcastic waiter. Kermit manages to hold the gang together, even when being stalked by a harassing frog leg–selling restaurant owner.

When the car breaks down in the middle of the desert, Kermit is left with a group of scared and confused companions. They lose hope that their dreams will ever come true, and they reach out to Kermit for answers. Kermit, overwhelmed, gets defensive. Later, he goes for a walk and has a long, reflective discussion with himself. His feelings of responsibility overwhelm him, and he argues that he never promised the group anything. He reminds himself that the gang wanted to come not because they believed in Kermit, but because they believed in their common dream of making people happy.

Kermit picks himself up and returns to his band of lost misfits.

• • •

Leadership can be tough for frogs and humans alike.

If ever there was someone who seemed unlikely to be a leader, it was the apostle Peter.

Of the 12 disciples, Peter (also called Simon Peter) was one of the first Jesus asked to join Him. As Jesus was passing by the Sea of Galilee, He called out to Peter and Andrew, two poor fisherman brothers. He told them to leave everything behind and follow Him if they wanted to become fishers of men. Peter did, no questions asked.

Jesus forever changed Peter's life that day on the sea. He knew Peter was going to be a major force in spreading His message to the world. One day, Jesus said, "Now I say to you that you are Peter (which means 'rock'), and upon this rock I will build my church, and all the powers of hell will not conquer it" (Matthew 16:18-19).

Before becoming a great Christian leader, though, Peter had his fair share of bumps in the road.

PETER DOUBTED

Peter called to him, "Lord, if it's really you, tell me to come to you, walking on the water." "Yes, come," Jesus said. So Peter went over the side of the boat and walked on the water toward Jesus. But when he saw the strong wind and the waves, he was terrified and began to sink. "Save me, Lord!" he shouted.

MATTHEW 14:28-30

One evening, Jesus went up a mountain to pray by Himself while His disciples went ahead of Him across a lake. Later that night, while their wind-battered boat was still a long way from land, they saw Jesus walking toward them on the water. Jesus invited Peter to walk to Him. Peter got out of the boat and began walking on the water, but he soon grew fearful and began to sink. He cried out to Jesus to help him, which Jesus promptly did. But Jesus also scolded him for his lack of faith.

PETER WAS PRIDEFUL

Peter took him aside and began to reprimand him for saying such things. "Heaven forbid, Lord," he

said. "This will never happen to you!" Jesus turned
to Peter and said, "Get away from me, Satan! You
are a dangerous trap to me. You are seeing things
merely from a human point of view, not from God's."

MATTHEW 16:22-23

Near the end of His ministry, Jesus revealed to His disciples that
He must travel to Jerusalem, where He would suffer, die, and rise from
the dead. Peter refused to believe Him—and he even berated Jesus for
speaking the words. Jesus once again had to put Peter in his place for
thinking he knew better than God.

PETER GAVE IN TO FEAR

Peter denied it in front of everyone. "I don't know what
you're talking about," he said. Later, out by the gate,
another servant girl noticed him and said to those standing
around, "This man was with Jesus of Nazareth." Again
Peter denied it, this time with an oath. "I don't even
know the man," he said. A little later some of the other
bystanders came over to Peter and said, "You must
be one of them; we can tell by your Galilean accent."
Peter swore, "A curse on me if I'm lying—I don't know
the man!" And immediately the rooster crowed.

MATTHEW 26:70-74

While Jesus was being accused and beaten in the high priest
Caiaphas's home, Peter waited outside in a courtyard. A servant girl
remarked that he had been in the company of Jesus. Peter flew off the
handle in a panic and denied that he knew Jesus—not just once, but
three times before the rooster crowed, as Jesus predicted he would. He
was ashamed of himself and wept.

Yeah, Peter had a rough start.

The world has certain expectations for leaders. They're expected to
be commanding. Charismatic. Powerful. They need to know all the
right answers and the right people. They must sidestep mistakes with
ease (and the perfect sound bite). It also helps if they photograph well
for an election poster.

Jesus says that to be a true leader, none of that stuff matters. He said, "Among you it will be different. Whoever wants to be a leader among you must be your servant, and whoever wants to be first among you must become your slave. For even the Son of Man came not to be served but to serve others and to give his life as a ransom for many" (Matthew 20:26-28).

Often, the best leaders don't look like the political figures on election posters. They are servants. They are bold, but kind. They pick people up and show them the way.

Eventually, God sculpted Peter into exactly His kind of leader.

God used Peter for leadership in mighty ways, despite Peter's setbacks and character flaws. He was a devoted, passionate believer from the moment he chose to follow Jesus. He knew who Jesus truly was right from the start. He was the first one to call Jesus the Son of God, the Messiah:

> He asked them, "But who do you say I am?" Simon Peter answered, "You are the Messiah, the Son of the living God." Jesus replied, "You are blessed, Simon son of John, because my Father in heaven has revealed this to you. You did not learn this from any human being" (Matthew 16:15-17).

After Jesus's resurrection, He commissioned His followers with a specific task:

> "Go and make disciples of all the nations, baptizing them in the name of the Father and the Son and the Holy Spirit. Teach these new disciples to obey all the commands I have given you. And be sure of this: I am with you always, even to the end of the age" (Matthew 28:19-20).

Peter shook off his previous blunders, bucked up, and took this commission to heart. He...

...was the first one to preach to the crowds on the day of Pentecost (Acts 2).

...performed a miraculous act of healing in the name of Jesus (Acts 3).

...suffered threats and beatings to proclaim the good news of Jesus (Acts 5).

...was the first one to bring Christ's message to non-Jewish people (Acts 10).

...preached that God does not show favoritism—He loves everybody (Acts 10:34).

Leaders are responsible for making decisions that affect others. They lead others to change. They draw people toward a common goal. In Peter, God developed important leadership qualities like boldness, confidence, humility, integrity, and assertiveness. And just like Kermit, Peter gathered others around a common goal, but Peter's goal was sharing Christ's love.

Peter had his flaws, true. But because of his stumbles, he could identify with the failures of other people. He knew what it was like to doubt or lose your temper, and his weaknesses were used to show God's ability to transform. From an arrogant and brash fisherman to a humble and willing servant, Peter showed us how God can use any one of us for His glory.

God can raise a great leader from *anywhere*—from a sea in Galilee to a swamp to your hometown.

Is He calling you to lead?

Grab your banjo and go.

27

NEW LIFE
WARM BODIES

Anyone who belongs to Christ has
become a new person. The old life
is gone; a new life has begun!
2 CORINTHIANS 5:17

f I like anything even less than toilet rats, it's zombies.

Ellen does not like zombies.

Ellen does not like zombies.

(One more time, for clarity's sake.)

ELLEN DOES NOT LIKE ZOMBIES.

Night of the Living Dead, The Walking Dead, Dawn of the Dead, Zombieland, Shaun of the Dead... I want no part of them. Some people might think my zombie embargo is because of the brain eating. But honestly, that's not it. I'm from the South, and I'm German. I've seen people eat some pretty weird stuff, like pork rinds and bratwurst and boiled peanuts, so who am I to judge?

No, my real issue is that zombies

    do

        not

          stop.

They are relentless, and that displeases me.

No good plan exists for combatting zombies. You can run. You can hide. But zombies just keep coming, like a Black Friday shopper at Spatula City. What's that, you say? *You* have a plan? You'll drive your car to a nonzombie territory? Honey, you are going to run out of gas eventually, exposing you to gas-station zombies—and, oh, by the way, *there is no nonzombie territory*. You plan on waiting them out? Don't be ridiculous. Please. Zombies are the undead sloths of waiting you out. We've already discussed this: Zombies don't stop.

You really have no plan.

What's worse is that a few years ago some new storytellers got the brilliant idea to make zombies superfast, like in the movie *28 Days Later*. As if frothing, lumbering zombies weren't bad enough. It's like when you go to the store and see that they're now making pumpkin spice soy milk. The original soy milk was nasty enough, and now you have this to contend with.

I just don't like any part of this zombie business.

Well…wait, I take that back. I do have one little zombie exception: a zombie named R.

The sweet movie *Warm Bodies* is a different kind of zombie story. A zombie *love* story, to be exact. It sounds implausible to use the words *zombie* and *love* together, but *Warm Bodies* proves it can be done.

R is a zombie. He can't remember how he became a zombie, or why he's wandering around the airport, or why he sometimes feels empty and lonely. He can't even remember his first name, only that it started with an *R* in his former life. He collects relics of his humanity—like a Guns N' Roses record and a snow globe—in an abandoned airplane. He thinks he's missing something from his undead life, but he lacks the ability to process what it could be.

One day, while he's out looking for fresh meat, R meets Julie, who is *not* dead. She's out with a band of living humans, scavenging the wrecked city for supplies like food and medicine. As soon as R's zombie pack gets a whiff of these fresh humans, they attack. During the ambush, R takes one look at Julie and is smitten. Instead of eating her, he saves her from his band of zombies and takes her home to protect her.

Reaching R's airplane hangout, Julie is scared out of her mind—but also dumbfounded. Having been raised by a stern, military father, she was taught to hate zombies with a passion. She's under strict orders to kill zombies on sight because of the hopelessness and depravity of their condition. Yet here she is—hanging out with a zombie who plays music, covers her with blankets, and scavenges for canned fruit to feed her. R is just different.

Although she's wary, Julie begins to trust and care for R, and her friendship seems to have a restorative effect on him. His color comes back. His speech and mind begin to clear. He smiles.

As much as she is surprisingly enjoying R's company, Julie knows she must return to her military-sieged home in the city. Her dad will be looking for her. R is brokenhearted, but he agrees to take her back. As they're attempting to leave the airport, the other zombies corner her to attack. R swoops in to protect her, and Julie reaches out to hold his hand. The zombies stop dead in their tracks, transfixed by Julie's small gesture. A spark of transformation begins in them as well.

Julie returns home and misses R terribly. R returns home and misses Julie terribly.

But something is brewing. The really bad zombies—the Boneys, zombies who have lost their remaining shreds of humanity—don't like the renewing change occurring in the zombie world, and they blame R and Julie. R realizes he must find Julie and let the humans know the regular zombies are changing *and* warn them about the Boneys. R has a tiny problem—Julie lives behind a well-protected fortress with her zombie-hating father—but that's not going to stop him.

R secretly weaves his way into the barricaded city to find Julie. Julie scolds him for risking his "life," but she's clearly delighted to see him again. After giving R a humanizing makeover, they attempt to approach her father to persuade him to give the zombies a chance. *This doesn't go well.* R and Julie are now on the run from both the Boneys and her father's militia.

They run through the top floor of an abandoned stadium, but the Boneys corner them on a ledge. Their only way out is to jump off the landing into a shallow pool far below. R holds on to Julie and jumps, using his body to shield her from the impact of the fall. After they gather themselves, Julie realizes that she loves R and she kisses him.

Unfortunately, Julie's dad uses their tender moment as an opportunity to shoot his daughter's new boyfriend. While Julie is pleading with her father to spare R, she notices a miracle. Something mysterious has happened to R. He's bleeding. Zombies don't bleed. R is alive.

Julie's love has turned R back into a living, breathing, loving human.

Julie's father finally opens his eyes and admits he was wrong about R. The humans join forces with the zombies to take out the rest of the Boneys, who are too far gone to save. The humans begin to start relationships with the zombies, and slowly all of the zombies return to life.

Warm Bodies might be the only zombie movie in history where love conquers death.

But that's exactly what love does.

• • •

We, too, were once dead. Not our bodies, but our souls.

In Ephesians 2:1 and verses 4 and 5, Paul writes, "Once you were dead because of your disobedience and your many sins…But God is so rich in mercy, and he loved us so much, that even though we were dead because of our sins, he gave us life when he raised Christ from the dead. (It is only by God's grace that you have been saved!)."

Paul knows a thing or two about being born again. He was living the life of a good-looking zombie. Before he was Paul, he was Saul. Saul had everything going for him, according to the world at the time. He had been born to a devout Jewish family in Tarsus, an influential port city in modern-day Turkey. He was born a Roman citizen, which carried a great deal of weight back then. He was also a Pharisee, a law follower.

On the outside, Saul looked stellar. But on the inside, he was dead.

When we first meet Saul in the Bible, he's the designated coat checker at the stoning of Stephen, a follower of Jesus (Acts 7:58-60). While Stephen preached of salvation in Christ, Saul watched as the mob killed the disciple. He didn't stop there, either. He began persecuting Christians himself—entering house after house, dragging both men and women off to jail. He was out for blood, all in the name of religious law.

One day Saul was on his way to the city of Damascus to see if he could find more Christians in Jerusalem to jail. Suddenly, he was blitzed by a blinding light. Then, Acts 9:4-6 tells us,

> He fell to the ground and heard a voice saying to him, "Saul! Saul! Why are you persecuting me?"
>
> "Who are you, lord?" Saul asked.
>
> And the voice replied, "I am Jesus, the one you are persecuting! Now get up and go into the city, and you will be told what you must do."

His traveling buddies were beyond confused because they hadn't seen a thing. Adding to his bewilderment, Saul was also now blind. I Ie got up, and his friends led him to Damascus. Once there, he holed up in the home of a man named Judas. For three days, he prayed and didn't eat or drink.

A disciple of Jesus's named Ananias was in Damascus too. The Lord told him to go find Saul and lay his hands on him so he could regain his sight. Ananias was understandably hesitant:

"Um, God? So…wasn't this guy coming to jail all of us?"

God promised him it was cool. He had specifically chosen Saul to preach the gospel to Jews, non-Jews, poor people, kings—everybody. That was good enough for Ananias, so he did what he was told. Ananias found Saul and laid hands on him, and Saul's sight was healed. He was instantly filled with the Holy Spirit. He jumped to his feet, was baptized, and then ate a big meal.

Almost immediately, Saul, who by Acts 13 was called Paul, began proclaiming that Jesus was the Son of God. He preached in synagogues and meeting places. He talked to anyone who would listen. He didn't need to be coaxed into this new life of his; he was on board the moment he met Jesus on the road. He was alive again.

The other Christians were initially suspicious. I mean, this was the guy who had hunted and threatened them, and they were used to being on their guard against him. It was like a reformed zombie striding up to you and saying, "Listen, I know I wanted to eat your brains last week, but I swear I'm a vegan now." For good reason, the apostles had reservations.

But a man named Barnabas took a chance on Paul. He saw that Paul's conversion and love of Jesus were genuine. He urged the other Christians to accept him into their family, and they did.

From that point on, Paul
   could
      not
         stop.

He was driven to share his good news with the entire world, so he just kept going. He preached. He wrote letters. He healed the sick. He organized churches. He traveled to different countries, town after town, proclaiming the gospel of Jesus. He was attacked, harassed, threatened, jailed, yelled at, and chased out of town. But he didn't care.

Christ's love had brought Paul back to life, and Paul wanted the same thing for everyone else.

We each have our own rebirth story to share, and each story is unique.

Your rebirth might not have occurred with a blinding flash of light. (Or maybe it did. But I'd be really impressed if it involved a disco ball of some sort.) Your story might be dramatic and full of twists and turns, or it might be quiet and subtle. Maybe it's even funny.

Whatever it is, your story is yours alone. And it's powerful.

God wants you to tell it, so tell it. Tell everyone about the wonderful way He brought you back to life.

28

LOVE
WALL-E

We love each other
because he loved us first.

1 JOHN 4:19

T he other day while I was driving, I stopped at an intersection. I
looked over and saw that someone had taken a white Sharpie to
the stop sign there and changed it to read "Never STOP Loving."
I stared at it for a while and pondered its deep message.

Then someone honked at me, so that was the end of that.

I think the subject of love fascinates most humans. Maybe not the
impatient dude behind me, but yes, most of us. From street signs to
movies to books to skywriting to marriage proposals on a jumbotron,
we're drawn to love stories.

I think that one of the sweetest tales of love can be found in the
Pixar classic *WALL-E*.

In the distant future, after nearly destroying earth with garbage and
pollution, humans have vacated the planet to live on a space barge. All
that remains on earth are a trash-compacting robot named WALL-
E (Waste Allocation Load Lifter: Earth-Class) and his pet cockroach.
Day after day, WALL-E dutifully does his job: gathering and stacking earth's waste into tight little bales of trash. His only respite from
his loneliness is collecting remnants he deems his "treasures": a spork,
a Rubik's Cube, a tiny sprout. One of his pastimes is watching an old

VHS romantic musical over and over. WALL-E yearns for a hand to hold, for someone to love.

One day, something changes in WALL-E's solitary world. A new robot named EVE (Extra-terrestrial Vegetation Evaluator) arrives, looking for plant life. WALL-E is immediately smitten. He begins to follow her around, determined to win her over. At first, EVE is irritated by WALL-E's continued presence, but his sweet nature finally breaks down her cool exterior.[1] Unfortunately, this happens at precisely the same moment she finds signs of life on earth—WALL-E's sprout—and automatically switches into hibernation mode.

WALL-E is devastated to lose his new friend, but he's still determined to take care of her, no matter what. He protects the motionless EVE from the elements, takes her on dates, and remains loyally at her side. When the mother ship comes back to retrieve EVE and the sprout, he refuses to be parted, clinging to the side of the shuttle.

EVE awakens when she returns to the space barge. At first she's horrified to discover that WALL-E has followed her back to the ship. She is a singularly focused robot—her prime directive is bringing the plant life to the ship's captain to place the vegetation in a Holo-Detector to trigger a hyperjump back to earth for recolonization. Her directive seems to supersede any fondness she might feel for the endearing robot. But WALL-E loves EVE so much that if the directive is important to her, it's important to him as well.

He attempts to help EVE bring the tiny plant to the captain, despite battling the main ship's nefarious autopilot computer and its minions at every turn. During their escapade, EVE finally grows to appreciate WALL-E's devotion, and she falls in love with him.

Finally, so EVE can complete her directive and humanity can be saved, WALL-E sacrifices himself to help bring the plant to the Holo-Detector. EVE is brokenhearted for WALL-E, but she's determined to save her love. After the ship is launched back to earth, she returns to WALL-E's home to locate spare parts to fix him. She frantically pieces WALL-E back together, but, alas, his memory is still shot. His sweet WALL-E-ness is gone.

---

1. Literally. Because she's a robot.

Sadly, EVE gives WALL-E one last kiss…and miraculously, that kiss is just enough to zap WALL-E back to his former self. EVE and WALL-E are joyfully reunited. The humans and their robot friends begin to rebuild life on earth, and they all live happily ever after.

• • •

As a single person, I can relate to WALL-E, especially when he's in his earth-tidying years. Like WALL-E, I'm just kinda doing my solo thing right now. I keep busy. I find new passions and pursuits. I clean up my little people's messes quite a bit. I hang out with my "cockroach" sisters and friends.

But also like WALL-E, I still want a hand to hold.

I wasn't always single. I started out single, of course, as we all do. Then in adulthood, I wasn't single for quite a few years. Then stuff happened. Then there I was, back to being single again and full of grief. Finally, after years of praying and therapy and turmoil battling, I'm in a good place.

If anything, I think I hold love even *more* precious now that I've experienced heartbreak and disappointment. I still think love is amazing and to be held in high regard. When I see examples of real love in everyday life—a husband and wife laughing together, a sweet kiss from a toddler, a bear hug from a friend—I treasure it and tuck it away in my heart. I'm still convinced love is a very, *very* good thing. I'm thankful that pain didn't turn me into a bitter person or harden my heart toward love. That would have been a tragedy.

It's easy to become jaded toward love, though. I think a big part of the problem is that our world today sets up a false standard of what real love looks like. It tends to focus on passionate, romantic love, but not even a realistic view of *that*. It's rare that you get to see a glimpse of kindhearted, sacrificial love, like in the movie *WALL-E*. (I find it ironic that one of the best cinematic examples of true love is between robots.)

Television, magazines, websites, movies, and books—they tend to show love as being intense and passionate. Hollering at each other, like Scarlett O'Hara and Rhett Butler. Tricking each other, like Lucy and Ricky Ricardo. Impatient, like Romeo and Juliet. The world wants us to see the only desirable love as being obsessive, jealous, selfish, and, sometimes, just plain mean. Even some beloved animated fairy tales are thinly veiled stories of psychological torture. I mean, for Pete's sake, *Beauty and the Beast* is the musical version of Stockholm syndrome.

It gets confusing when the love message doesn't match the actions. Most characters really shouldn't say, "I love you" at all. It would be more accurate to say, "I'm obsessed with you." "I'm emotionally abusing you." "I minimally tolerate your presence." Or "I lust for your body, and I couldn't care less about everything else."

Those stories might make our heart beat faster, but they don't show real love.

With so much exposure to love impostors, real love can seem boring. Our view can be so warped by dramatic, crazy, fake "love" that we don't recognize the real thing anymore.

We must go back and rely on what God tells us love is. If you want an accurate description, read 1 Corinthians 13:1-7, where Paul paints a portrait of what true love looks like:

> If I could speak all the languages of earth and of angels, but didn't love others, I would only be a noisy gong or a clanging cymbal. If I had the gift of prophecy, and if I understood all of God's secret plans and possessed all knowledge, and if I had such faith that I could move mountains, but didn't love others, I would be nothing. If I gave everything I have to the poor and even sacrificed my body, I could boast about it; but if I didn't love others, I would have gained nothing. Love is patient and kind. Love is not jealous or boastful or proud or rude. It does not demand its own way. It is not irritable, and it keeps no record of being wronged. It does not rejoice about injustice but rejoices whenever the truth wins out. Love never gives up, never loses faith, is always hopeful, and endures through every circumstance.

Sometimes we just need a wake-up call to remind us what love *really* looks like, so we can take a pass on the fake stuff.

Real love is patient.
>Love doesn't pressure or force its agenda.
>Love is willing to wait.
>Love doesn't throw a fit when it doesn't get its way.

Real love is kind.
>Love doesn't call you mean names.
>Love doesn't sulk and manipulate.
>Love treats you gently.

Real love is not jealous.
>Love doesn't stalk or harass.
>Love is happy to share.
>Love is respectful of boundaries.

Real love is not arrogant.
>Love isn't full of itself.
>Love doesn't boast or brag.
>Love isn't a big ol' jerk.

Real love is forgiving.
>Love doesn't hold a grudge.
>Love doesn't give the silent treatment.
>Love gives new beginnings.

Real love rejoices with truth.
>Love is honest.
>Love wants you to be the best you can be.
>Love cuts through the nonsense.

Real love endures.
>Love stays through the messes.
>Love makes sacrifices.
>Love keeps going when everything else falls apart.

Yes, choose the good stuff because real love is amazing.

Deep down, I do believe some hunky Jesus-loving geek is out there for me somewhere. I have a feeling God is working with him through some hard stuff and refining him, just as He's been doing with me. My dude will need to have a merciful heart and a good sense of humor to tackle a project like me. I hope he also knows how to pick up his own socks by this point in his life. And that he likes cooking dinner, because I hate cooking. Or maybe we can just order pizza every night.

But even if it's just me for the rest of my life, I'm good. I do have love in my life. I have the most *important* love—God's love. He treasures me. He is patient and kind to me. He sacrificed His Son for me.

He never STOPs loving me.

29

HARDSHIP
MINECRAFT

I have told you all this so that you may have peace in me. Here on earth you will have many trials and sorrows. But take heart, because I have overcome the world.

JOHN 16:33

There once was a girl named Ellen
Who did not understand Minecraft.

"A MINECRAFT LIMERICK"
BY ELLEN ELLIOTT

A ctually, that's more of a statement than a limerick.

But it's true. I do not get Minecraft.

Is it a game? Virtual reality? A colossal waste of time? I have no clue.

I *do* know it causes the children who hover in the peripherals of my life to go crazy. They devour books about Minecraft. They attend Minecraft summer camps. They would probably be lining up for Minecraft tattoos if not for adult intervention.

One day, I asked my Minecraftaholic nephew to explain it to me.

"Bleep bloop Stampcat yada diamond blocks sniff snorf,"[1] said the nephew.

---

1. Paraphrased explanation to spare the reader from enduring the long, actual explanation.

"Oh," I said. "So it's like a virtual Lego world with blocks. Kind of educationally architectural. How nice."

"Except when you go from Creative Mode to Survival Mode. Then zombies try to kill you."

"Hold up, there," I said. "WHAT?"[2]

So *basically*, as far as I can decipher, here's the Minecraft breakdown for the rest of us:

Creative Mode: *La la la.* Let's build a nice square house and live here happily ever after with our little square llamas.

Survival Mode: *La la la.* Let's build a nice square house and…ZOMBIE ATTACK! LAVA DESTROYS ALL THE THINGS! CREEPER ASSAULT! LIVESTOCK DYING FROM STARVATION! LLAMAS FALL INTO ENDLESS PIT OF BLEAK NOTHINGNESS!

Why anyone would want to play in Survival Mode is beyond me. Out here in the real world, we get quite enough Survival Mode already, thank you very much. That's *all* we've got. Every moment of our lives is played out in Survival Mode.

One man who knew Survival Mode quite well was Moses.

• • •

If you take a brief walk through the life of Moses, you'll see it wasn't a lovely stroll through Central Park. During his lifetime, Moses was…

> …born a Hebrew male slave, under the rule of an Egyptian pharaoh who killed *all* Hebrew male slave babies. Not a great start.

> …placed in a homemade basket, alone, along the bank of the Nile River. Granted, it was to ensure his survival, but still. Rough.

> …adopted and raised by Egyptian royalty, yet loyal to his Hebrew roots. He watched with discomfort as his

---

2. Remember: Ellen does NOT like zombies.

biological relatives were abused and oppressed by his adoptive relatives.

...forced to flee Egypt for Midian after he killed an Egyptian guard who was beating a Hebrew slave.

...chosen by God to become the voice and leader of the Hebrew people, despite his extreme reluctance because of stuttering issues.

Moses also...

...confronted a brutal pharaoh and unleashed plagues upon his country of birth, including frogs, locusts, rivers of blood, and other nastiness.

...parted the Red Sea to help his people escape the Egyptian army. (You can't tell me that wasn't one long, muddy walk. In *sandals*.)

...wandered the desert for 40 years with a bunch of ungrateful whiners who were prone to worship idols and wax poetic about their former days of slavery.

As a final kicker, after all of his hardships, Moses wasn't allowed to set foot in his longed-for promised land because of an unfortunate disobedience incident involving his staff, a rock, and some water.

Moses's life is a prime example that we were never promised a rose garden. Jesus warned us that we *would* have trials and challenges throughout life. None of us is exempt. Throughout the Bible, not even God's special messengers were spared from hardship. When you choose to follow God hard core—*really* choose to live for Him and follow His adventurous plans—you're guaranteed a wild ride. This world isn't going to always be pretty or easy or comfy.

But.

That's not what the world wants you to think. With all its news, advertising, movies, television shows, media...well, the world makes promises very different from God's. It tries to convince you that if you just buy the right house, have the perfect job, marry the spouse of your dreams, or fold your clothes a certain way, all your troubles will be over. Perfect peace. No more hardship. No more Survival Mode.

It's a lie. This world *is* tough. Our real-world "zombies" are things like poverty, persecution, and sickness. Just when one zombie is thwarted, here comes another one, lumbering toward you, bearing a new threat, like unemployment or scurvy. Survival Mode ends only when you start your eternal life in heaven.

Thankfully, despite the adversity of the world, our God is a merciful God. Even Moses, a man with a life full of hardship, was shown mercy, time and time again. Like…

> …when his mother was miraculously able to hide him—a crying, sniffling, laughing, pooping, loud little baby—from the Egyptian guards. That's a serious miracle right there.

> …when he was placed in the Nile River, his sister, Miriam, was by his side.

> …when his adoptive Egyptian princess mother chose his own mother to become his nanny.

> …when God sent his sister and brother to help him because he was scared to return to Egypt to save the Hebrew people.

> …when his people were saved from the worst of the plagues—the death of all firstborn sons—by marking their homes in lambs' blood, allowing God's wrath to pass over them.

> …when he was wandering through the desert. His people were provided quail, manna, and dew.

> …when, although he wasn't allowed to set foot in his

beloved promised land, he was allowed to gaze on it with his own eyes before his death. Even when God disciplines, He is kind.

God is merciful with you as well. He gives you soft landings from the hard falls. He stays with you during your periods of sadness and grief, never leaving your side. He mends your broken heart after it gets stomped to smithereens.

Yes, life is full of hardships, but it's also full of God's love.

30

UNITY
THE AVENGERS

The human body has many parts, but the many parts make up one whole body. So it is with the body of Christ.

1 CORINTHIANS 12:12

'm not a fan of group projects, mostly because I'm a card-carrying introvert.[1] I like to work alone most of the time. I do like having people around in my general vicinity because I like General Vicinity People, but I also like those General Vicinity People to stay out of my personal beeswax.

In other words, I like you, but I'd like you better if you stood over *there*.

When I'm assigned to a group project, I just groan.

My worst group project was in college when we were instructed to film a music video. One bossy girl railroaded the whole assignment, as is apt to happen on group projects. I vaguely remember a grunge band lip-synching to terrible music while court jesters skipped through a water fountain. I don't remember much more, because I spent most of the time hiding behind a pillar. Hiding behind pillars is what introverts do best.

Group projects are a tricky business, even for superheroes.

In the movie *The Avengers*, danger has again befallen the earth. The Marvel Universe is filled with radioactive mutants or power-hungry

---

1. Yes, we have a club. No, we don't have any meetings. Or group projects.

alien villains, insisting on destroying civilization, but this time the villain is Loki. (In case you're wondering, the villain is Loki quite a bit of the time. In fact, if there's ever a question about who's causing trouble, just assume Loki is involved. Most likely, you will be correct.)

After Loki steals the Tesseract and begins plotting to destroy the universe and what have you, the agents of S.H.I.E.L.D. (Strategic Homeland Intervention, Enforcement, and Logistics Division—earth's homeland security) realize they might need more than just one superhero this time. The only problem? Superheroes tend to work alone.

The powers that be decide to crack open a dormant project called "The Avengers Initiative": a team of the world's greatest crime fighters. They attempt to bring together the potential members, one at a time:

- Captain America, a U.S. military-created WWII supersoldier

- Iron Man, the arc reactor-powered, metal-suited creation of the snarky and self-confident billionaire Tony Stark

- Thor, a mighty, hammer-wielding "god" of Thunder from the realm of Asgard (and also Loki's brother)

- The Black Widow, a lethal spy assassin from S.H.I.E.L.D.

- The Incredible Hulk, the green, impulse-control-impaired alter ego of the brilliant, mild-mannered scientist Bruce Banner

- Hawkeye, a guy who shoots arrows

When the superheroes are first brought together, the result is pretty much what you'd expect from so many strong-willed personalities vying for control: sheer chaos.

At first, nobody can agree on *anything*. Everyone has a different opinion. Everyone wants to be in charge. Thor wants to take Loki as prisoner back to Asgard, and he doesn't have any intention of being a team player. His initial meet and greet with Captain America and Iron Man becomes a forest-decimating melee. The gang calms down long enough to load everyone onto S.H.I.E.L.D.'s Helicarrier airbase, but the discord continues.

Before long, Captain America and Iron Man discover they have different leadership styles. What's more, neither one likes the other. They squabble with each other. They squabble with their S.H.I.E.L.D. bosses. They squabble-squabble-squabble until the Helicarrier comes under attack by Loki's alien allies. And then the Hulk just hulks out all over the place, and everything gets smashed to pieces.

The Black Widow battles the Hulk. The Hulk battles Thor. The Black Widow battles a mind-controlled Hawkeye.[2] Loki escapes.

Yes, the Avengers are a total disaster. Not only is nothing getting done, but because of their team's internal struggles, their primary mission of saving earth from destruction is in serious jeopardy.

• • •

Sometimes the same kind of nonsense happens within our Christian community. Divisiveness can and does plague our spiritual family, especially when selfishness takes over.

Some examples of not getting along include:

• backstabbing
• gossiping
• underhanded scheming
• condemning members for their failures
• putting down "lesser" members
• praising and overcompensating the members with more visible roles
• mocking members who are a little different

It's sad that this kind of behavior isn't new; it's been going on for a long time. Paul was dealing with strife and conflict in the early years of the church, and one church needed a swift kick in the tush. The new church in Corinth was having major problems. Bickering, jealousy, and legalism ran rampant, and the news made its way back to Paul.

2. He shoots some more arrows.

Paul needed to get through to his fellow Christians, to emphasize how important it is that all of us find a way to get along and work together. In 1 Corinthians 12:18-26, he writes,

> Our bodies have many parts, and God has put each part just where he wants it. How strange a body would be if it had only one part! Yes, there are many parts, but only one body. The eye can never say to the hand, "I don't need you." The head can't say to the feet, "I don't need you." In fact, some parts of the body that seem weakest and least important are actually the most necessary. And the parts we regard as less honorable are those we clothe with the greatest care. So we carefully protect those parts that should not be seen, while the more honorable parts do not require this special care. So God has put the body together such that extra honor and care are given to those parts that have less dignity. This makes for harmony among the members, so that all the members care for each other. If one part suffers, all the parts suffer with it, and if one part is honored, all the parts are glad.

In our Christian body, we have so many parts, all different. And that's fabulous! The church wouldn't work if we were all the same. But things get out of whack when certain body parts start thinking they're more important than others. It's really a bunch of baloney. We're all needed and valuable. Many Christian communities have shattered because their members just couldn't appreciate one another.

When we're all working together, it's a joy to see the body operating as it was meant to function. Our body includes:

Hands

...those who minister, help, and serve others

Ears

...those who listen to the troubles of others

Eyes

> ...those who see what's really happening and can discern good and evil

The Mouth

> ...those who speak truth to others

Knees

> ...those who are fervent in prayer

Feet

> ...those who share the love of Jesus, far and wide

Fellow geeks, I'd like to take a moment to speak directly to you.

Sometimes it might feel like you're a random body part—one of those parts that seems to lack clear purpose. Maybe it's a body part that seems purely decorative or even nonsensical—like the belly button, the uvula, or the appendix.[3] You might feel like there's no place for you in the body of Christ because you're a little odd. I've felt this way about myself many times.

But God made you *too*. You add zest and humor and funkiness to the body, so rock your little uvula self! Do your thing for God, whatever that happens to be.

It's time that we, as a Christian community, value all the distinct parts in the body of Christ—no matter the function. But that starts with you trusting God about your part. You must step up, value yourself, and be who you are.

The Avengers also finally came around and realized they had to work together. They rallied and defeated their foes (pretty much destroying New York City in the process) once they realized they were greater than the sum of their parts.

So are we, my Christian family. Work together.

---

3. Hawkeye is totally the appendix of the Avengers.

31

LEGACY
DOCTOR WHO

Not that I was ever in need, for I
have learned how to be content with
whatever I have. I know how to live on
almost nothing or with everything. I
have learned the secret of living in
every situation, whether it is with a full
stomach or empty, with plenty or little.

PHILIPPIANS 4:11-12

Here's a joke I once heard:
> How many artists does it take to screw in a lightbulb?
> Just one, as long as the world keeps revolving around him.

Bwahahahahahaha.

Oh, calm down, artists. I kid because I love.

Truly though, throughout history, artists have been the source of much intrigue and fascination. They are often the ones walking off the beaten path, seeing life through a unique perspective.

Doctor Who meets one such famous artist in the *Doctor Who* episode "Vincent and the Doctor."

Doctor Who is a British television series that has been in production, off and on, since 1963. The premise revolves around a character called the Doctor, a Time Lord who can travel through space and time. The Doctor travels in a stolen time machine known as a TARDIS (Time and Relative Dimension in Space), which happens to look just like an ordinary blue British police call box from the outside despite its vastness on the inside. The Doctor is a strange sort of being. He's centuries old, but he can regenerate his body.[1] Although he can visit any planet at any time, he's fascinated with Planet Earth and human beings. And since the Doctor likes to travel with company, he regularly chooses an earthly companion for his travels.

In the episode "Vincent and the Doctor" (Season 5, Episode 10—since the revival), the Doctor and his current companion, Amy, are in the Musée d'Orsay. They are admiring the artwork of Vincent van Gogh, the famous impressionist painter, in a wing of the museum devoted entirely to his art. As the Doctor closely studies one of his paintings, he becomes perplexed by a creature he sees lurking in the background art. He realizes it's imperative that they pay a visit to the artist himself in 1890 rural France. To Amy's delight, they race their time machine to meet Vincent van Gogh.

When they find him, he's living in ridicule in the small French town of Arles. He resides in a shack, filled to the brim with unsold paintings. Vincent is lonely and depressed, and he views his life as an utter failure. Yet he continues to do the only thing he really believes he must do: paint. Finding a kindred spirit in Amy, Vincent quickly attaches himself to his time-traveling guests. He offers his services to them as they search for a fearsome alien creature, a Krafayis, which only Vincent can see with the naked eye. Meanwhile, Amy struggles with the knowledge that, in only a short amount of time, Vincent will succumb to his depression and end his life.

After "defeating" the invisible monster in an old church (a touching scene where we learn that the monster is simply blind and frightened), Vincent is saddened that his new friends will be leaving him. The Doctor and Amy decide to take Vincent back to the present-day museum so he can see the legacy of his life's work. As he enters his wing of the Orsay, he's overwhelmed with emotion and pride. He hears a museum

---

1. Regeneration only happens when the Doctor is hurt or dying. Not on a whim, like say, when he's got a big ugly pimple. Not even a Time Lord has power over a big ugly pimple.

guide praising his artwork and referring to him as the greatest artist ever. He cries with joy.

The Doctor and Amy return Vincent to his home. As they part ways, Amy is hopeful that the experience will have been enough to break through Vincent's loneliness and prevent his tragic death. The duo returns to the present-day museum and discover that, unfortunately, their friendship did not alter Vincent's sad ending.

Amy is brokenhearted. She thinks they didn't make a difference in Vincent's life, but the Doctor disagrees. He tells Amy that life is full of both good and bad, but their relationship certainly added more good to Vincent's short life. He also points out that the monster is now missing from the church painting.

At the end of the episode, Amy notices that a famous van Gogh sunflower painting now has a dedication: "For Amy." She laughs… and cries.

● ● ●

I think we all wonder about our legacy from time to time, just as Vincent did.

Will my work and efforts make a difference? Or will they all be forgotten, like yesterday's jam? Will anyone be changed because of my time on earth?

We don't have the luxury of a time machine to hop into the future and check out the results of our efforts, but how do we choose to live life when faced with the question of our legacy?

I think we can benefit from looking at the life of Brother Lawrence.

Brother Lawrence was born Nicolas Herman in France's Lorraine region. Historically, not a lot is known about his beginnings. He was born into poverty around 1614. He joined the military at a young age, mainly to have the basics in life, like food and a bit of money. He ended up serving in the Thirty Years' War, a religious war fought in Europe from 1618 to 1648. After being injured, he left the army and served as a footman for the treasurer of the king of France.

At age 26, he joined a Parisian Catholic monastery called the Discalced Carmelites (*discalced* means "barefoot"). He changed his name to Lawrence of the Resurrection and began serving the community and his fellow monks. At first he feared his brothers would be irritated by his social awkwardness, but that wasn't the case. He was a delight to everyone who knew him. The only reason we know anything about him at all is because of the recorded conversations of people who flocked to keep him company or corresponded with him through letters. These letters and conversations turned into a small, simple book titled *The Practice of the Presence of God*.

Brother Lawrence spent most of his monk service in the kitchen of the monastery, in charge of washing the dishes. At first, he wasn't so keen on this assignment, but he quickly discovered that it pleased him greatly. It gave him time to think, pray, and worship God. He truly believed that his real job—the only one that mattered—was loving and delighting in God all day long.

He was content with his small life because he could focus on God's love. His life seemed to embody the verse "You will keep in perfect peace all who trust in you, all whose thoughts are fixed on you!" (Isaiah 26:3). At the core, Brother Lawrence was happy to be living every moment of the day while basking in the knowledge that he was a beloved child of God. His joy was so powerful and infectious that it transcended the 80 years of his life on earth. Centuries later, his wisdom and joy are still being passed along, pointing people to Jesus.

And all he really did was wash dishes.

The truth is, we just don't know what mark our lives will leave after we're gone. We can set out with what we think are high and noble purposes, but only God knows how things are going to go down. Those grand plans you think are meant to change the world might not turn out to be so important after all. The important thing might turn out to be simply spending an afternoon fishing with a child. Big plans are often not nearly as significant as those small, daily actions that God calls us to do.

For instance, in writing this very book, I don't know what impact it will have. I'm hoping more people than just my mother will read it. But I don't even know that. Mom is pretty much into Tom Clancy these days. You, dear reader, might wind up being the only person who reads this sentence. Maybe you're the only person meant to read it.

Yet I know I was called to write it, so write it I am.

Ultimately, we're called to live our lives one day at a time, loving God and loving other people. Jesus gave us our primary mission: "'You must love the LORD your God with all your heart, all your soul, and all your mind.' This is the first and greatest commandment. A second is equally important: 'Love your neighbor as yourself.' The entire law and all the demands of the prophets are based on these two commandments" (Matthew 22:37-40). But sometimes we're also called to clean pots and pans. Or paint beautiful paintings. Or write books.

We don't always know God's purpose in His leadings, or what the result will be when we follow. But if He is calling us, we can rest in the fact that He is using our efforts for His glory—whether we get to see the outcome in this lifetime or not until our eternal life.

We don't need to worry about our legacy because God is using us to paint a beautiful picture of His love.

ABOUT THE AUTHOR

Ellen Elliott lives in Arkansas with her two children. She likes writing, illustrating, cartooning, and sculpting. She doesn't like math, brussels sprouts, or running.

She still has no superpowers.[1]

Visit her at **www.thereignofellen.com**

---

1. Except for the fly-swatting thing.

Looking for a New Way to Geek Out?

Ellen Elliott wants to share her love of list-making with you! Experience fresh joy every day when you create lists that encourage prayer, reflection, and gratitude. Combine list-making with your daily pursuit of the heart of God in this beautifully illustrated and thoughtfully designed journal.

Get the gist?

Now, go forth and list!

To learn more about Harvest House books and
to read sample chapters, visit our website:

www.harvesthousepublishers.com

HARVEST HOUSE PUBLISHERS
EUGENE, OREGON